At David C Cook, we equip the local church around the corner and around the globe to make disciples. Come see how we are working together—go to **www.davidccook.org**. Thank you!

transforming lives together

What people are saying about …

Courageous

"Terra Mattson is the real deal. She not only speaks from experience as a mom and as a professional counselor but also stands on a mountain of research and biblical wisdom. We've followed her work for years and are thrilled to see her put this message into such an accessible and practical book. If you have a daughter in your life, you need this book."

Drs. Les and Leslie Parrott,
New York Times bestselling authors of
Saving Your Marriage Before It Starts

"We have served families, adolescents, and children for four decades and have never seen the challenges we are seeing today. If there was ever a time mothers needed an engaging, biblically, and culturally astute guide for parenting girls, it is now. Terra has blessed mothers and daughters with exactly such a book. *Courageous* is filled with practical insights and wisdom delivered in a very engaging style."

Dr. Steven and Celestia Tracy,
founders of Mending the Soul

"Terra Mattson has written a book for every woman who is ready to face her fears, fight for her dreams, and show her daughter how to live the very same way. With grace and skill, Terra shows us the possibilities that exist as women sink their roots deep into the love of God while keeping their arms outstretched to a broken world. It's a beautiful, hopeful picture, indeed."

Bo Stern-Brady, author of *Beautiful Battlefields,*
pastor, and founder of She.ology

"One of the most life-giving guides for helping young women learn to winsomely follow Jesus in a post-Christian culture. Terra's years as a licensed professional counselor make this biblically anchored book relatable and applicable, providing many practical how-tos for flourishing in grace."

Dr. Bruce McNicol, president and cofounder
of Trueface, coauthor of *The Cure*, and
executive producer of *The Heart of Man*

"I believe that, through what is taught and modeled in this book, both mothers and daughters will experience principles of love, grace, and relationship that will profoundly lay the foundation of courage, hope, and purpose in their lives."

Bill Thrall, cofounder of Trueface
and coauthor of *The Cure*

"Reading *Courageous* encouraged me deeply—what a marvelous resource for all who hear God's challenging command to raise children in the way and grace of the Lord. It's written especially for mothers, but fathers must read it too. Terra's godly wisdom flows from her life as a faithful student of God's Word, a mom in a complicated world, and a marriage and family counselor who has seen it all."

Gerry Breshears, PhD, professor of theology
at Western Seminary in Portland, OR

"If you are a mom who is looking for one practical resource to guide your daughter through her developmental maze from pre-adolescence to healthy womanhood, this is it. *Courageous* is truly one of the best books I have ever read that combines biblical truth with authentic, relatable action steps for moms with young girls.

Terra Mattson weaves her beautiful warmth and wisdom into every page as she vulnerably shares her own journey while inviting moms to follow her lead in raising empowered, godly, wise, and courageous world changers!"

Michelle Watson, PhD, LPC, radio host of *The Dad Whisperer* and author of *Dad, Here's What I Really Need from You*

"I have known Terra Mattson for more than twenty years. The wisdom and insight of this book come from personal experience, the hard work of learning, hours of coming alongside others as they seek to grow, and careful attention to the wise insights that come from research and education. She has provided a highly accessible and helpful road map for helping women of all ages thrive and flourish in a world of increasingly confusing and mixed messages. Let those desiring to raise up a next generation filled with grace and courage pay attention."

Steven G. W. Moore, PhD, executive director of M. J. Murdock Charitable Trust

"This book takes an honest look at the complicated worlds of being a daughter and being a mother to these young ladies. Terra brings a unique perspective—as a mother and a psychotherapist—to the challenging issue of being a mother and a daughter in today's confusing world. *Courageous* brings an honest look at the importance of courage and grace, and I encourage Christian mothers and daughters to share in its practical wisdom."

Daniel Sweeney, PhD, LMFT, LPC, professor of counseling at George Fox University, practicing therapist, and ordained minister

"Terra weaves her personal experiences as a mom with her professional knowledge as a therapist in this insightful book. It will empower you to raise the next generation of girls with skills to thrive in a complex world. She is the warm and wise friend we all need as we navigate the challenges of parenting."

Tristen and Jonathan Collins, authors of *Why Emotions Matter*; Tristen is a trauma therapist, and Jonathan is cofounder of The Bible Project

"*Courageous* convinces me of an unblemished reality, that God adores me, as I imperfectly adore and love my daughters. This mix of truth and application allows me to face hard things with grit, hope, and joy. God is excited for you to experience this kind of love in your family."

David Pinkerton, dad in Phoenix, AZ

"I opened *Courageous* to grow as a mom. It resulted in a raw but grace-filled journey of growth as a daughter, which has impacted every part of my life."

Bethany, mom of three children in Seattle, WA

"My biggest fear was to be the mom of a daughter, knowing how broken I was. *Courageous* validated so much in me. This book continues to be a resource that I go to as a mom of a Courageous Girl and to be a Courageous Girl myself!"

Jen B., Courageous Girls mom and leader in Portland, OR

Courageous

Courageous

being daughters rooted in grace

Terra A. Mattson
MA, LMFT, LPC

DAVID **C** COOK™

transforming lives together

COURAGEOUS
Published by David C Cook
4050 Lee Vance Drive
Colorado Springs, CO 80918 U.S.A.

Integrity Music Limited, a Division of David C Cook
Brighton, East Sussex BN1 2RE, England

The graphic circle C logo is a registered trademark of David C Cook.

The website addresses recommended throughout this book are offered as a
resource to you. These websites are not intended in any way to be or imply an
endorsement on the part of David C Cook, nor do we vouch for their content.

Details in some stories have been changed to protect
the identities of the persons involved.

Library of Congress Control Number 2019944564
ISBN 978-1-4347-1262-2
eISBN 978-1-4347-1263-9

© 2020 Living Wholehearted, LLC
First edition published as InCourage: Raising Daughters Rooted in Grace by Living
Wholehearted Publishing in 2018 © Terra A. Mattson, ISBN 978-1-949709-00-1

The Team: Michael Covington, Rachael Stevenson, Grace Humphreys, Susan Murdock
Cover Design: James Hershberger

Printed in the United States of America
Second Edition 2020

1 2 3 4 5 6 7 8 9 10

112019

To my daughters, who are the inspiration for everything I write—this book started with you in mind. I wanted to write something that you could hold on to as you develop into women. Keeping the end in mind, I pray that you will someday hear the heartbeat of my mothering in the pages of this book and live out its message of grace.

Contents

Foreword   **15**

Preface: About Courageous Girls   **17**

Acknowledgments   **19**

Introduction: The Reality of Being a Girl   **23**

1. She Walks with Confidence   **35**

2. She Embraces Holy Crap   **51**

3. She Feels to Heal   **69**

4. She Tunes In to the Voice of Grace   **95**

5. She Knows Who She Is in Community   **115**

6. She Makes and Keeps Friends   **141**

7. She Is Fearless ... Almost   **165**

8. She Is His Beloved   **185**

9. She Dreams ... Big   **211**

10. She Practices Rhythms of Rest   **227**

Starting a Courageous Girls Group   **249**

If You Enjoyed This Book   **253**

Scriptures about Identity   **255**

Notes   **259**

Foreword

As a mom of three grown daughters; a grandma to several grand-children; a pastor's wife, ministering over the years to junior high and high school girls as well as women; and founder of Divine Threads, a ministry reaching out to disenfranchised women, I could not be more excited about Terra's book, *Courageous*.

Courageous could be one of the most important books you will ever read if you are a woman, especially a mom or a daughter. Terra bravely steps into subjects that need to be addressed, not only personally for each of us but also together with our daughters. In a time in history when our identities are threatened on a daily basis, we need voices louder than our culture telling us the truth of who we are and what we need. *Courageous* does this in very practical ways, giving us both clinical as well as biblical information.

Thank you, Terra, for being a woman of courage, willing to step into very difficult subjects with our daughters. May our culture be changed, one girl at a time!

Kathy Towne
Founder of Divine Threads, Portland, OR

Preface

ABOUT COURAGEOUS GIRLS

This book is a supplement for Courageous Girls groups and is written especially for the mamas who lead and participate in them. However, you do not need to start or join a group in order to benefit from the principles and wisdom found in these pages. You may not even have a daughter but find yourself drawn to process your own story as a woman. We were all little girls at one point, right? Within these pages, you will find hope, help, and healing that will transform your understanding of what it means to live well. Know that this resource stands alone, though you will find many connections to the Courageous Girls material woven into the chapters.

I knew the importance of living in community and walking side by side with other moms after I gave birth to my two girls, yet I found the business of life was always competing with the ideals of my heart. I started Courageous Girls in 2012 for my own daughters and for our local community. God had more in mind, and a movement of Courageous Girls groups started popping up in other parts of the country and now the world. Mamas heard about the significance of Courageous Girls groups and started asking for help. In 2017 I realized that this format and curriculum needed to be available to help mothers navigate the systemic issues plaguing our girls today. With the help of Aimee Eckley, a curriculum developer, and the moms of my first Courageous Girls groups, mycourageousgirls.com was published as a free resource for any mom and daughter who want to grow in courage and participate in a Courageous Girls group.

Courageous Girls is an online curriculum equipping moms and daughters to have regular and committed gatherings that foster confidence, resilience, and grace-filled relationships over a long period of time. Utilizing an ongoing process that incorporates both biblical and clinical inspiration, moms and daughters who participate in Courageous Girls will know the depth and breadth of God's love for them, discovering their unique value and purpose along the way. Having regular discussions in safe and personalized environments from early elementary school through high school promotes the development of authentic and strong relationships between girls, between mamas, and, most importantly, between mothers and daughters. Consequently, these communities help us understand our unique beauty as women so that we can stand rooted in grace, identity, purity, purpose, resilience, and courage no matter what life brings.

Instead of isolation, Courageous Girls choose community and connection. Instead of worldly input, we seek God's Word in our lives. Instead of competition, comparison, and judgment, we grow in gratitude, joy, and acceptance so that we are equipped to love others well and live from a place of wholeness and grace. It is not a meager task; it is one that requires sacrifice, strength, character, and commitment. It is a process that is constantly evolving, especially in our ever-changing, technologically infused lives. As our daughters grow and change, we too must adapt the way we connect with them as well as the way we demonstrate love. May you be inspired and encouraged to become a Courageous Girl.

Acknowledgments

Have you ever birthed a baby and recalled all the many supporters who carried you to the finish line? This book was years in the making, and I have been overwhelmed by the gift of encouragement I have received in birthing this "baby."

To my husband, Jeff, who not only is my best friend and business partner but has been the power and faith behind all my dreams—you have helped put feet to my passions. I am so grateful for the ways God loves me well through you. Not only do you keep me laughing and enjoying the little things in life, but you also see me in the middle of all my mess. See how much I love you.

To my parents, Superpops and Nana (aka Saint Lou), who laid the foundation for who I am today—your commitment to each other and to my sister and me throughout our growing years launched me into living a life of intention. You gave me confidence to be myself, resilience to face hardships, love to hold my feet steady, and fond memories that have become bedtime stories for my girls. Mom, you were the first in my life to model what it means to be a Courageous Mama. The influence of your lives will touch more people than you will ever know. Here's to staying cool, calm, and collected. *Baeza!* And to my courageous sister, Tiffani, who exhibits many of the principles of this book, thank you for letting me in and for the gift of your laugh! It's the only one that still makes me wet my pants.

To my Courageous Mamas, Alicia B., Alicia K., Ambria, Beth, Heidi, Hollie, Janelle, Jodee, Lisa, and Rachel, who said yes to the crazy idea of a Courageous Girls group—thank you for walking with me as we navigate raising our girls. My unique friendships with each of you have given color to these pages. Your prayers are forever woven into the ripple effect of these words. Thank you for loving me well and allowing me to let my hair down.

To my mother-in-law, Muzzy (and her husband, Papa), thank you for your prayers, for your generosity in hosting many years of Courageous Girls retreats, and for fostering our Courageous Girls relationships as moms and daughters. You have been an incredible source of support and encouragement over the years. Here's to Julia Child impersonations, Muzzy's Marvelous Manners, and modeling the life of a courageous woman.

To Aimee Eckley, who stepped out in faith when asking me whether I would want to get the message of Courageous Girls out to more moms—your willingness to pray, brainstorm, edit, and put countless hours into the Courageous Girls website and curriculum was a catalyst to close the loop for this book. Your fast friendship has been a testimony to how God uses the various gifts of His people for a common purpose.

To my mentors, community, friends, and prayer team—especially Kathy and Christina—your investment has given me a sense of strength, courage, and peace as Jeff and I step out into deeper waters. I am forever grateful for the ways you have freely fanned the flame of our lives and offered wisdom, discernment, and faithful friendship over many years.

To my clients, thank you for your courage to face the reality of your lives, to step into the process of healing, and to trust me with the most sacred places of your story. You have taught me more than I could ever say in one book and remind me daily of the ways God redeems our pain.

Thank you to our Living Wholehearted team, who partner with us to rebuild, restore, and renew healthy relationships. It is such a joy to shoulder this work together.

To Bill Thrall, Bruce McNicol, and David Pinkerton with Trueface and my tribe at David C Cook, thank you for your guidance and belief in this project.

Finally, a humble thank-you to God, who not only loves me but by grace also uses me to love others. *Your power is made perfect in my weakness.*

Introduction

THE REALITY OF BEING A GIRL

Growing up as an American girl in today's culture takes extraordinary courage. Yet it seems that the youth of this generation have increasingly fewer of the traits needed for the challenges before them. The message to "be more," "do more," and "fake it" is pervasive in our nation. From magazine stands to social media messages, from television to textbooks, from our churches to our homes, these messages reflect a condition of our society: we cannot stop striving to gain or greaten our "success." Despite our efforts, our society is not succeeding; we are more depressed, anxious, addicted, self-destructive, and selfish than ever before. We are raised to believe that gaining material success, staying young, remaining healthy, and forming lasting relationships will bring happiness; the truth is, all these things fail us. None of them provide lasting security; though they may cascade in a season, they always run dry over time.

As a mental-health provider and ministry leader with over twenty years of experience, I have witnessed the negative effects of our culture on girls and women of all ages through the stories they share with me. I have been blown away by the story lines they recount, many of which depict the same plot with different characters. In other spaces where people often feel safe to share their experiences, such as educational settings, the stories abound as well. Their lives resemble many of the narratives of my closest friends, my neighbors, and even my own daughters. So often we think the worst-case scenarios happen only to others. Yet we must know that all of us share in these stories.

I recall one client, a fourteen-year-old, quietly telling me about numerous boys who had approached her for nude pictures. She shared her stories with a brash tone intended to declare her value; to her the sheer number of boys conveyed her high value among her teenage peers. Like many parents, her mother and father justified her phone as a necessary and convenient communication tool and trusted her to make good choices. They told her that sex before marriage is a sin, but the conversation ended there. Her private Christian school, filled with kids who wanted to please their parents, teachers, and God, was far from equipped to hold this young girl's hand as she walked through the thornbushes of life. Despite having a good heart and a solid upbringing, she eventually sent pictures of herself unclothed to a boy, who shared it with other male classmates. This increased the pressure to engage in oral sex with several boys whom she "sort of liked." As I listened to her story, my heart broke because she mirrored the experience of many other girls who explore these challenging situations alone—not because her parents did not care but because they were simply unaware.

Another young client of mine shared how she could not stop obsessing over photoshopped Instagram pictures while she counted the calories she put into her body. She cried internally as her dad regularly made jokes about women in public and shamefully commented on female bodies on TV. She secretly battled bulimia, and her primary role model in life, her mom, battled her own demons around controlling food. She felt trapped in a world that indirectly communicated that worth can be attained only through a certain kind of beauty. Though she loved God, she struggled to know if He loved or even liked her in return. How could God love a girl who was not perfect? He has favorites, right?

Young girls are not the only ones affected by the pressures of modern American culture. A suburban mom shared her story in my office. Like many other women, she told me that she finds herself dreaming of a different marriage each evening after she puts her three kids to bed. She routinely ignores her husband, a workaholic who binges on TV and escapes to pornography late at night, and she finds solace through fantasizing about the lives of others on Facebook and HGTV. Masking depression and panic attacks behind a carefully made-up face, she leads Bible study and mentors young couples in church. A few glasses of wine in the evening take the edge off her exhausting, lonely life, and she prays that her daughters will have better marriages than she has. She recounted that she feels trapped and alone.

A strong woman shared with me—the first time she had told anyone—how she was pursued by her high school PE teacher eight years ago when she was in her teens. Though other girls gossiped about her sexual engagements with this instructor, no one offered her help. She never knew how people found out about their relationship, but she felt tremendous shame because of their glances and whispers. The teacher, trusted by the community, fed off the girl's distorted view of love: he paid attention to her, which made her feel special. By disguising his sexual abuse as a fulfillment of her own romantic fantasy, he coerced her into a sexual relationship that left scars on her heart and filled her with lies of worthlessness. Even after the relationship ended, she found herself attracted to men who treated her abusively. Ironically, she is an advocate for sex-trafficked girls but cannot see the connection between herself and the survivors she helps in ministry. On the outside she is a performer whom the world views as a remarkable woman with a bright future. Like the other women whose stories I've shared, she wears the mask well, taking it off only in the sanctuary of my office.

Something has to change.

Today American girls and women are living divided lives. We are living in a reality described by the ministry Trueface as the "Room of Good Intentions."[1] This is a space where we try really hard to be good people and do good things while wearing masks and embracing false identities. In wearing masks, we avoid the depths of our own humanity and miss the essence of our purpose: to be firmly rooted in grace. Grace transforms us from the inside out, not by our own strength but by God's power and through His love. This is what I want to cultivate in my own family, our community, and our culture.

The Room of Good Intentions has led to a dismal state of affairs for the girls and women in our nation. Middle school girls are exploring oral sex as a "safer" form of sex. The average American girl has had intercouse by the time she is seventeen, and by nineteen, three-fourths have already had sex.[2] Sometimes girls in our culture lose their virginity at the hands of multiple partners simultaneously. By the time a woman graduates from college, she is likely to have experienced one form of sexual assault or abuse, regardless of her background. A recent study conducted by the Harvard Graduate School of Education found that 87 percent of women aged eighteen to twenty-five reported having experienced sexual harassment in their lifetime; many report that they have never talked with their parents about how to avoid these situations.[3] Our girls are engaging in risky behaviors. Too often a girl's "No" holds little power, as many boys and men have been led to believe she does not mean it.

Instead of actively teaching girls from a young age to use their voices boldly, society communicates that they should attract and maintain others' love and affection. Social media, selfie culture, and instant fame through venues like YouTube, Snapchat, Instagram, and reality television have created in little girls a deeply rooted desire to grow into something big. Unfortunately, the message to be great is rarely taken to mean they should aspire to be rocket scientists, cure finders, or great teachers. Instead, the media platforms that engage our youth promulgate the seeming ease and simplicity of becoming an instant internet sensation. You need only amass a certain number of followers and tweets for the paid promotions and sponsors to foot the bill for life. The danger in girls accepting and believing this cultural truth is the acceptance of the lie behind it: if you are not *somebody*, then you are a nobody. This is so far from God's heart.

In a world that offers immediate gratification, one's ability to cope (known as resilience) with anything less than constant satisfaction has plummeted. The rise of self-harming behaviors such as cutting, eating disorders, pornography addictions, and even suicide are at the highest rates across many age groups—and they are rising still. These behaviors are the spoiled fruits from the branches of depression, anxiety, comparison, and loneliness. As I counsel women and girls of all ages, the fear of missing out and not being enough is extraordinary. The pain is palpable; they feel stuck between competing demands: loving themselves, their families, their friends, and their significant others while maintaining an image put forth on social media. This affects not only young girls but also grown women, who find themselves trapped in these struggles despite having life experience, perspective, and fully developed brains.

Increasingly, younger girls enter the offices of trained professionals across the country to learn how to manage their emotions and conquer the unbeatable game posed by the Room of Good Intentions. It is an epidemic: one in three girls is sexually abused by a trusted person in her life; one in two girls thinks her ideal body weight is less than she weighs; every female has been affected by the cultural norms of being pretty.[4] You may be tempted to believe that this is an exaggeration; doing so certainly makes it easier to maintain the status quo. Based on my years as a therapist, I actually would argue that the numbers are far greater than we know. Over half the women I work with experienced some sort of covert or overt sexual abuse before the age of eighteen. Most of my clients have shared this truth only inside the sacred space of counseling; statistics are based on reported abuse that can be quantified and documented publicly.

The reality is that the sex and pornography industries loom over our homes, destroy our marriages, and teach our children that we are merely animals driven by our uncontrollable visceral and primal needs. One needs only to review the ticket sales at the box office for the *Fifty Shades* series to confirm that sex sells. While most women feel nauseated at the thought of being reduced to their bodies and branded for others to admire and use for their own personal gratification, we still get caught up in the net cast to catch us and pull us in. We spend billions on beauty products, gym memberships, and, my personal favorite, chin and buttock reconstruction—but for what? So that we will be loved? So that we will be seen? So that someone will notice our beauty and fulfill our longing to be cherished? I believe that what we really (albeit secretly) need to confirm is that we are not alone in our feelings of insecurity and lack of power. We are all in the same boat and need a way out.

Mamas, get these statistics into your heads! Tear away the veil of indifference or the mantra that you replay in your head that "that's not my daughter." Ask yourself, with brutal honesty, *What habits do I engage in that foster feelings of inadequacy in my daughter(s)?* It is not easy to identify our shortcomings or weaknesses. However, the cost of avoiding dealing with our own way of being in the world is painstakingly high—and our daughters' resilience and strength depend on it! This book is not meant to scare you into paralysis—quite the opposite. I hope you will be empowered to act and move toward love in order to grow strong and resilient yourself. This is what will help our daughters: being raised by mamas who are actively engaging with them and teaching them how to live through life's hardness and filth, holding God's hand every step of the way.

Ladies, you are more than you could ever imagine! You are *not* what society tells you to be. You are *not* what a film producer suggests you should be. You were beautiful and worthy from the moment you were born. You were created with purpose, and the love and meaning you long for is freely available and willingly given by your God.

I think loneliness is at the root of most, if not all, unhealthy coping behaviors. When we are confused about who we are and we try to make meaning based on the human experience alone, the depths of our souls remain empty. God created us for relationship from the beginning. His triune character—Father, Son, and Holy Spirit—reflects a Creator who is relational within His very being. As the Genesis account of creation tells in chapters 1–2, we are made in our Creator's image with a desire to be connected. The digital world we live in has made us globally connected, but the relationships are held together by a thread, and our care for one another has become very fragile over time. This will be addressed further in chapter 10. The point is that our girls are growing up with moms who are lonely and lost too. We desperately need to redefine how we link arms as moms and pursue our daughters in a way that penetrates their God-made souls.

It is time for a movement. Are you in?

You might be thinking, *Yes, but how?*

I get it. Much Christian help is offered with platitudes (*Just pray and trust …*), but it often doesn't explain the crucial next steps. Similarly, most clinical research and self-help books offer just that: self-help. A self-help approach is far too limiting. Without something greater than ourselves, we miss the richness of Scripture and all God has to offer us. This book aims to fill in the gaps that Christian advice and self-help approaches create by unraveling *how* girls develop a confident voice, a strong sense of self, and a lasting spiritual depth that keeps them rooted throughout the storms of life. Integrating empirically proven clinical wisdom and facts about human development, trauma research, and play therapy with healthy spiritual formation, this book explores the theories, principles, and tools you can apply to your ordinary rhythms of life. Soaked in a foundation of biblical truth, my heart is not only to give you a vision for who you and your daughter are meant to be but also to help draw a road map that weaves transformational principles into the fabric of your relationship.

No one is left out of the pages of this book. Walking with others for many years, I have sat with all kinds of people: prostitutes, pastors, single moms, attorneys, models, surgeons, homemakers, CEOs, Millennials, African Americans, Asian Americans, Latin Americans, Middle Eastern Americans (my own heritage), college students, graduate students, farmers, grassroots advocates, nonprofit founders—you get the idea. Despite our differences, there are fundamental experiences we all share. Regardless of our upbringing, every girl and woman longs to be seen, loved, and cherished. Being raised in a Christian home does not guarantee this will happen. According to Bill Thrall, cofounder of Trueface, the truth is that unless our theology transforms our reality, our children will have a skewed understanding of Father God.[5]

At the ripe age of twenty-eight, I became a mom. I had been to four years of college, had finished graduate school (focused on healthy child and spiritual development), and had worked in ministry and clinical environments, helping other families with health and healing. Yet nothing prepared me for the gut-wrenching vulnerability that came with knowing all the pain and suffering that my child could endure in this world. I felt so powerless to help her. With prayer, Scripture, and all my training in relational health and trauma recovery, I wanted to drive this road differently. I even prayed that my children would have just enough dysfunction so that they understood the sorrows in this world but not enough that it paralyzed them and kept them from living abundantly and having an impact on their world. I begged God to hold me tightly as I held my baby tenderly in a world of people who would seek to use her and discard her heart.

As a woman who found my own voice (and started using it) just before I birthed my daughter, I wanted her to recognize her own voice early on—to understand her thoughts, feelings, needs, and desires. I wanted her to be able to advocate for herself and others who did not have a voice. I was determined to help my daughter become a girl who knew her value. When my second daughter was born less than two years later, I knew I had been given an enormous task. I prayed this same prayer again, showering her with the same pleas. It was out of this cry that Courageous Girls was born.

When my oldest daughter was in first grade, I made an intentional effort to invite a few other moms into this grand adventure. To my surprise, they said yes! To this day, we are still venturing together, trying to navigate the world of raising girls who know they are loved and who love others well.

Movements start with one voice declaring "It's time." William Wilberforce, one of the voices in Britain's slave trade abolition movement, said, "There is no shortcut to holiness; it must be the business of our whole lives."[6] Raising daughters who have a sustained relationship with a personal, loving, and grace-filled God—and who know their purpose in life—requires more than just hope or routine attendance at Sunday morning church services. It requires more than just solid self-esteem and a good education. It requires even more than just parents who love their children. Those things are important, but what is really required is laying down our lives for our daughters—entering into their world to support them and committing ourselves to becoming Courageous Girls alongside them.

The God of the Bible models sacrificial empathy; He left heaven and entered our world through the person of Jesus. This is the same God who rose from the dead and who, as the Holy Spirit, resides inside every mom who follows Christ. So wherever you are starting, whatever your story, bring all of yourself to the table. You are the key to your daughter's courage. The good news is that the journey of raising our girls is not one we have to walk alone. Instead, we can be empowered by God to accomplish this work as we root ourselves in His grace. Paul's prayer for the church in Ephesians comes from the same heartbeat that provides life to me and mamas everywhere:

> I pray that out of his glorious riches he may strengthen you with power through his Spirit in your inner being, so that Christ may dwell in your hearts through faith. And I pray that you, being rooted and established in love, may have power, together with all the Lord's holy people, to grasp how wide and long and high and deep is the love of Christ, and to know this love that surpasses knowledge—that you may be filled to the measure of all the fullness of God.
>
> Now to him who is able to do immeasurably more than all we ask or imagine, according to his power that is at work within us, to him be glory in the church and in Christ Jesus throughout all generations, for ever and ever! Amen. (3:16–21)

This passage has influenced me throughout my adult life. As a young adult of twenty years old, I was conscious to make the most of every opportunity. Determined to avoid passivity, I fervently penned this prayer in my journal:

> *Lord, may You increase and I decrease (John 3:30),*
> *may Your power be made perfect in my weakness*
> *(2 Cor. 12:9), and may I not only live out the*
> *ministry of reconciliation (2 Cor. 5:18–19) but*
> *also know the riches of Your love that You may do*
> *far more than I could ever ask or imagine in and*
> *through me for generations to come (Eph. 3:20–21).*

This prayer, made up of verses that shaped my calling as a marriage and family therapist and my heartbeat for the greater church, continues to remind me how big God is. My faith is not dependent on me but rather on humbly watching God manifest Himself in the lives of ordinary people. Writing this book and developing Courageous Girls for my own daughters were never aspirations of mine, but they originated from the depths of my soul, compelling me to trust and obey.

I hope that the pages of this book will breathe life, hope, and vision in to you as a mother. If you have a Courageous Girls group or want to start one, this book provides deeper dialogue and ways for you to grow not only in your walk with God, yourself, and your daughter but also in your relationship with other moms. At the end of each chapter, you will find suggestions for ways to integrate the principles of this book into your daily life. May this book not only strengthen you but also equip you to understand fully what it means to be *in courage.*

Takeaway

Which struggle did you identify with most as you read about the stark realities women and girls face today? Consider these questions: *Am I truly willing to look deeper into my own way of being so that I can lead my daughter well? What currently stands in the way of transformation in my own life? Whom might I invite along in this journey?* Ask God to guide you as you read through the chapters, showing you specific principles that apply to your life.

Take It a Step Further

As you consider who your daughter is and who she is becoming, consider writing a prayer for her from your heart. Give the prayer to her and let her tell you what she might add to your prayer. Pray this prayer together. Consider committing to finishing this book. Consider discussing this book with other moms as part of your own courageous journey.

1

She Walks with Confidence

She is clothed with strength and dignity;
she can laugh at the days to come.
Proverbs 31:25

If you wanted to bring about a fundamental change in people's belief
and behavior ... you needed to create a community around them,
where those new beliefs could be practiced and expressed and nurtured.
Malcolm Gladwell, *The Tipping Point*

As you read this book, my prayer for you is that you would hear the heart behind it. No matter what you may struggle with as a mother or a daughter, I pray that you will know, without any shadow of a doubt, that you are loved. I believe that if you deeply understand *agape* love, everything else in your life will flow from that fullness. We can love others only when we ourselves are loved (see 1 John 4:19). We can give away only what we have received. Without love, daily life (and parenting in particular) feels painfully difficult. Christ came to bring us freedom; it is for the sake of freedom (freedom from self-condemnation, shame, fear, and bondage) that I hope you receive these words.

It takes enormous courage to love and be loved well—not the kind of courage we muster for daring acts, such as skydiving or swimming among sharks in the ocean's depths. Those are brave acts but not the variety that attracts everyone. The word *courageous* means many things in our culture today. Well-known author and sociologist Brené Brown defined it this way: "*Courage* is a heart word. The root of the word *courage* is *cor*—the Latin word for heart. In one of its earliest forms, the word *courage* meant 'To speak one's mind by telling all one's heart.' Over time, this definition has changed, and today, we typically associate courage with heroic and brave deeds."[1] I do not wish to speak about heroism or bravery. The kind of courage I discuss in this book comes from a deep awareness of who we are and to whom we belong. What if we knew that, because of our identity, we are *in courage*, so we do not have to produce it on our own? If we knew we always had a safe place to land, along with an endless source of strength, I believe we would be able to venture into unknown territories and live with greater meaning.

Recently, as I was having lunch with a friend and colleague, an elderly man approached our table. His thoughtful stare was noticeable; the skin around his eyes were covered with scars, telling a story of suffering. He held the rich wisdom of Oswald Chambers in his hand, a hint of abiding faith in old age. He spoke slowly, with steady intention, as if starting a sermon.

"In courage. In joy. To be in …" He wrapped a piece of paper around his arm, repeating the word *in* and affirming that courage, comfort, joy, and peace are found in the envelopment of God's love. He went on to say, "Enjoy. Encourage." His words flowed from the depths of his soul. If not for the prompting of the Holy Spirit, I might have passed this moment off as a lonely old man merely needing to be heard. However, something inside prompted me to pay attention. My friend and I thanked him for his wisdom, and I pointed to his worn book.

"Are your thoughts from Oswald?" I asked.

He looked me in the eye and humbly stated, "No, that was from God."

I smiled, goose bumps rising on my skin. He responded with a quiet grin, and through his crystal-blue eyes, I could see a story of one who had been misjudged and overlooked. As he turned to leave, I said, "Thank you and *in*-joy your day." I wanted him to know I had received his point.

A few minutes later he returned to our table to say, "Thank you for listening to my pearls of wisdom." Since I am typically addicted to efficiency and averse to interruption, my manifest patience was a sign of God's presence. "Of course," I replied with a smile. I was struck *again* by how the simple act of listening to another human being can make for holy moments.

What if we lived as if we were already *in* courage, content to *in*-joy this life, apart from our own expectations and the expectations of all those around us? What if we modeled this lifestyle for our daughters and they began to live the same way?

SHE GUARDS HER HEART

I believe this is the lifestyle of a Courageous Girl. Courageous Girls rest in God's love and keep in step with His way of abundant living. From a biblical perspective, this means she stays in touch with every piece of her heart. She has learned to care for it, nurture it, and recognize what Proverbs 4:23 says about it: "Above all else, guard your heart, for everything you do flows from it." In Old Testament Hebrew culture, the word we translate as "heart" is *lebab*, but it was associated with the core of one's being: mind and soul. Another way of expressing the idea might be to say a person's gut or innermost hidden parts. Many times we think *heart* refers only to one's emotions, but this is a Western interpretation. When we read this proverb in the Hebrew context, we recognize that we should treat our whole selves like treasured diamonds because all we do and say flows from whatever lies within us—from the core of who we are.[2]

My daughters have seen many of the inner workings of who I am—flaws and all. If you are a mom, I imagine you may identify with part of my reality: the cranky mom battling PMS or confronting the cacophony of chores calling to me from every corner of the house; the short-tempered mom snapping at my husband or struggling to regain composure after telling my girls the same thing repeatedly; the anxious mom, worried about a school event or work project; the fearful mom, troubled about finances and long-term security for my children. My children know what I look like before makeup and how many times I've worn the same outfit multiple days in a row. They have seen me act unkindly toward family members during disagreements and have witnessed me giving my husband the silent treatment when my feelings have been hurt. They have seen me grumble, set boundaries, overwork, and then crash. They have seen my pride enliven me like a roaring lion and paralyze me like a stubborn mule. They have heard harsh words fly out of my mouth before I could respond to the Spirit's gentle voice—*Be slow to speak and slow to anger* (see James 1:19). I have not always modeled what I hope my children will know deep down in their hearts—that my love for them will always burn brightly.

But in my broken humanity, my children have also experienced my sincere apology many times. Asking forgiveness from our children, genuinely and humbly, is a powerful route to connection and trust. This shows them in a tangible, experiential way how God loves us, how we can be restored when we have done wrong, and how to reconcile with one another. Following repentance, an actual change in behavior pushes me away from sorrow over mistakes made and propels me toward God. Yes, my children have seen my blemishes, but they also have experienced my desperation as I've fallen on my knees to hear the Lord. I desire for my daughters to see me wrestle with authenticity and vulnerability, both of which are difficult to cultivate and critical to healthy relationships. I secretly smile as they peek in on me and quietly sneak onto my lap for a cuddle as I'm curled up on the couch with my Bible, searching for God's heart, wisdom, and truth on good days and bad. I believe my daughters are experiencing me as a real person: one who is leaning in to love, surrounding my whole heart with both God and others, while being rooted in courage.

In our often routine daily lives—between laundry, dinner, basketball practice, gymnastics, dog walking, and homework—I hope my girls see me courageously standing up for those who are hurting. I want them to experience me loving deeply and grieving wholeheartedly. In the mess, I pray they see the beauty. My Courageous Mama prayer is that my girls (and your girls too) will see me (and you) modeling what it means to be a woman. The task is daunting, but I know God has honored me with it and therefore I must not take it lightly. Even more, I long to model for them the tangible ways that love overflows from the inside out; when I am filled with *agape* love, I am more likely to trust God's description of me as His child: "fearfully and wonderfully made" (Ps. 139:14).

We each have a little girl inside us who feels courageous and whom God created to reflect parts of His character to the world around us. We do not need to be perfect. We are not even meant to be "good girls" who make good choices all the time. Courageous Girls are far more than their decisions, actions, words, mistakes, failures, and flaws; we are more than our threshold for temptation, and we are more than our sins. My dear friend Dr. Michelle Watson, an author and the founder of the Abba Project, coined one of my favorite sayings: "My who is not what I do." Try saying it out loud; go ahead. No one is listening aside from that little girl living inside you. To take it a step further, my who is not defined by anyone other than God, Creator of my life. There is great power in freeing myself from my own expectations and comparisons with others. It may sound easy, but we know it is not. There is something in our female DNA that simply cannot resist checking out the woman in line in front of us and comparing ourselves to her. The urge to find fault with other women is real and often leaves us struggling to create authentic friendships and maintain healthy, fulfilling, and edifying relationships.

SHE VISITS ELI

Max Lucado wrote many of our family's favorite storybooks. One of the most frequently read books in our home is *You Are Special*.[3] It's about a town of wooden people who spend their days sticking dots and stars on one another. Those who make mistakes, are less attractive, or perform poorly compared with others receive gray dots. Those who are pretty or perform well receive gold stars.

The story's main character, Punchinello, is constantly covered with dots and feels unworthy. One day he meets a girl who does not have any dots or stars on her body, so he asks her to reveal her secret. Lucia tells him to visit Eli, the maker of all the wooden people. Punchinello visits Eli and finds himself at the feet of a loving carpenter who delights in his presence, despite Punchinello's dots. As Punchinello receives love from Eli, one of his dots falls to the ground. Eventually Punchinello learns there is no special formula for removing dots. Instead, relationship with the maker reminds each wooden person how uniquely special they are, and the security that comes from his love trumps the stickers' power and relevance.

Hopefully, you can see Lucado's metaphor. When we, as flawed individuals, spend time with our Maker, we are able to focus on how He values us and are less likely to possess self-limiting perspectives. While none of us enjoys receiving "dots" from our peers, it is certainly tempting to accept "stars" when they're being handed out—student of the month, player of the year, employee of the quarter; life has a way of keeping us tethered to stars with an ever-growing list of ways to earn them. Have you bought into this? Are you striving to earn the praise of another person? Are you working to excel at something so that you can achieve a higher rank or more publicity? Think in terms of our children's daily experiences. They have certainly bought into the world of stars and dots, undoubtedly because there is a deep hunger in our culture for stars. Why do they desire this kind of praise? Sadly, the more we hand out stars, the more our children thirst for them. Over time this thirst grows into an insatiable need that won't go away (no matter how many Instagram followers you get).

The serious problem with this mind-set is that we cannot have one without the other. By choosing to accept the stars when people offer them and proudly wearing the symbol so that others can see our "worthiness," we are, by default, posturing ourselves to accept the dots. We may try to refuse them, but they still stick. There is no shortage of dots, is there? We do not even need to list them; your mind (and likely your daughter's mind) is full of them already. Moms, heed this warning: it takes our children accepting only one dot to destroy the hundreds of stars they may have already accumulated.

As mothers, we work hard to fortify our girls with compliments. We teach that words can't hurt, though every one of us knows words can be like daggers. We try to armor them with the "right" clothes to wear to school to prevent verbal teasing or being left out. In trying so hard, we are still perpetuating the cycle of human-driven approval. Essentially, we hand out stars to our girls from birth in hopes of keeping them from receiving dots. In our society it's really hard to escape others' attempts to tag us with dots or stars (or, in the world of social media, thumbs-up or thumbs-down). Though this human approval system is not new, it has become instantaneous.

The sticker trap imprisons us in a performance-based cycle of rewards and consequences. Sometimes this approach is repackaged as the tenets of Christianity, the "shoulds" and "should nots" of the faith. But I am certain this is *not* what Jesus intended to impart to His people. Jesus never judged based on productivity levels or assessed people by their achievements. He did tell a parable about using our gifts and talents (see Matt. 25:14–30), but He did not keep tally marks of who earned stars and who received dots to determine the love and attention He offered. God does not have favorites, and His love is not based on our merits.

Let me clarify that words of affirmation and compliments *are* important. Freely offering life-giving words of encouragement is vital to healthy development. Every girl still needs to hear that she is beautiful, smart, generous, or kind—though her worth is not based on such attributes. When we gift our daughters with words that speak to their value, regardless of performance, they will be able to release the power of stars and dots.

So how do we help our kids find their worth based on their Maker's point of view alone? It starts with us—parents. We begin by teaching our children that their value is defined *only* by the unconditionally loving God who knit them in the womb (see Ps. 139:13). You can teach this directly or indirectly to your daughter but only if you accept the truth yourself. How you believe the Creator views you will translate to what you prioritize in your life. In a world that wrestles with priorities every second, we must remind our daughters (and ourselves) daily to return to the Creator—through prayer, meditation, singing, playing, reading His Word, using our talents to serve, and enjoying life. These are ways in which God intentionally pursues our heart. Remember, it is God's job to brush off the stickers that have been thrust on us. While we cannot control who tries to put stickers on us or our girls, we can determine whether or not the dots and stars retain their adhesive power. We do this by recognizing that we are created with purpose by a God who loves us and sees us as worthy through His Son, Jesus. The more we connect with "Eli," the more we can prevent the world's stickers from sticking.

Lucia, the female character in Max Lucado's story, is a terrific example of a Courageous Girl. She beautifully depicts one who chooses relationship with her Creator over definition by the other wooden people in her town. Lucia's relationship with Eli frees her to be all she is made to be. Sure, she stands out, but in doing so she points others to Eli so that they too can be free from the sticker trap.

The sticker trap burdens us with the three sabotages of true intimate relationship: shame, ego, and pride. In contrast, the Maker mind-set develops our resiliency against the temptation to accept outside judgments and pronouncements of worth. Developing Maker–mind-set resilience is hard to accomplish in today's world, but it is not impossible. The world is quickly changing, but the hard evidence of the great gospel message has never changed. I am confident that God's desire is not only to recognize our unmet needs but also to draw us close to Him, as daughters, so that we can be deeply loved. Our daughters will learn how to receive the love of God as they practice alongside us. We are their first picture of God as a relational, loving being.

SHE LIVES LIFE

As our children's primary caretakers, we are their first relationship models. Our relationships with our children communicate the loudest message of who God is and who they are. Our daughters will spend much of their adulthood either living out the messages we impart or trying to free themselves from them. Whether I am cuddling with my daughters on the couch or running around the house preparing for the next Courageous Girls gathering, I try to consider every moment an opportunity to disciple them. In all things, I am called to communicate and demonstrate the love of God to my family.

Here's the catch: I cannot be everything to everyone else *and* disciple my children well. No one can. Many try and fake it well for a while, but eventually something must be sacrificed on the altar of life. We try to juggle the endless demands and expectations of the world around us instead of stepping into the sweet spot for which we are uniquely designed. Competing priorities pull at us, promising that if we put our energies into certain endeavors, we will find fulfillment. Christians have even made up another set of standards that falsely promise, often through a 1-2-3 step plan, "If you …, then …" The truth is that there is *nothing* we can do to satisfy the world's expectations or guarantee outcomes, yet we still try. It's a dead-end trap to keep us frustrated and striving for validation. This way of thinking destroys us and distracts us from truly living.

In my life, letting go of this lifestyle has meant surrendering and accepting my specific call for today: to partner with my husband in our business; to see clients a couple of days a week; and to mother my girls intentionally through the treacherous waters of public school alongside a few other moms and daughters. I have stopped comparing myself with the blogging supermom and the Mother Teresa homemaker, though God bless them both!

For some moms, surrender means stepping down from a position at work. For another, it looks like working hard outside the home to make ends meet and put food on the table. For another, it looks like appreciating her marriage and small home while mothering three children and homeschooling. We do not need to do it all or be it all. We are called only to be our authentic selves, and it takes time to discover who that is. Social media will not tell us the answers but provides only ideas, inspiration, and, at times, sensory overload. We each have our own way of being the mom our girls need to see, and the only way we know our personal path is to spend time connecting with our own hearts and the heart of God.

Fill in the blank in the following sentence based on something that feels true of your experience: "If I am not _____, then I am not enough." Most of us can fill that space with several words that lead us to believe we are falling short. Here are some common answers: running my business well; attending the PTA fund-raiser; spending enough time with each child; sending out Christmas cards to my family and friends; providing permanent shelter for my children; fitting into my jeans; going to church; cooking a nutritious dinner every night for my family. The list goes on and on. How we answer this statement helps us determine where we find our identity and worth.

As you consider your statement, it's important to remember that lies, shame statements, and distractions are not the truth that God speaks over us. We are made in the image of God, and His uniquely ordained purpose rests on each of us. There is no other *you* on the planet. There is no one else like your daughter. Caroline Leaf, a brilliant Christian neuroscientist and author, said it this way while I sat in the audience at one of her lectures: "You make a lousy me, and I make a lousy you."[4] No matter what motherhood has stripped away from or added to your job description, no matter how many days end in tears while you kiss your baby's forehead because you arrived home after her bedtime, no matter what your neighbor posts on Facebook about the camps she sends her kids to in the summertime, you cannot live your life comparing yourself with others. The only way to settle this deeply human desire to compare ourselves is to turn our focus to God, follow what He calls us to do, and grow in the ability to celebrate what He is doing in others. It is so hard—but so good.

Get quiet. Can you hear God whispering? What purpose has He given you for this moment—not for tomorrow but for today? Here's the simplest way I can summarize God's response to me when I ask Him this question: to be courageous by being myself. It is a courageous act to be loved as I am and to love others as they are. I cannot do this perfectly, but when I can overflow out of my relationship with my Creator, I am enabled for courage. More importantly, I am equipped to engage the hearts of my daughters so that I can walk with them at every stage of life.

SHE LIVES IN TODAY

How do we know how to enter into relationship with our girls, especially if they are going through a difficult stage of development or struggling with issues we never experienced in childhood (hello, iPhones)? The world offers many suggestions and well-meaning manuals to address this question. Some parenting models allow children to experience life on their own—entirely independent of their parents, saying, "They won't learn unless they experience it themselves." An alternative extreme protects children from everything, so they enter the world without any life experiences outside those ordained by parents. Both philosophies leave our daughters vulnerable.

Following the wisdom of two of the world's leading experts in play therapy, Dr. Daniel Sweeney and Dr. Garry Landreth, I adhere to this approach: "Never do for a child that which she can do for herself."[5] This principle helps children develop deep inner confidence unrelated to the praise of others. This principle also teaches adults the importance of recognizing and educating ourselves about our children's current developmental stages. When we make ourselves attentive to our children, we can help them build skills and confidence, allowing them to practice new things or test new ideas within the safety of a relationship filled with love and limits. Being Courageous Mamas who invest in our Courageous Girls means each of us must take time to know our daughter's unique way in the world, help her build skills, and give her ways to practice and develop confidence within the safety and security of grace. This requires allowing extra time for mistakes, practice, and innovation.

To be truly honest, I struggle daily to prioritize this principle as well. Doing things for our children or missing an opportunity to come alongside them to encourage and train is far too easy in light of our busy lives. I still feel mommy guilt at times for doing something for myself or for serving various ministries instead of my family. I know the pressure to cook a nutritious meal so that my kids' memories of dinnertime are not only mac and cheese and reheated chicken nuggets.

Pausing long enough to look into my daughters' eyes at least once a day requires intentionality. I am slowly learning that living out who I am *and* being a Courageous Mama are one and the same. I am still in the process of learning how to accept that where I am is where I am supposed to be—a message I want all Courageous Girls to embrace. Grace meets us where we are and helps us grow from there.

There is so much to learn about being a daughter of the King of grace. The Bible tells us that each woman has purpose and is uniquely made and equipped to fulfill it. Her ability to fulfill that purpose is developed by spending time with God, sinking her roots into the truth that she is loved and boldly offering that love to others. This is what it means to be a Courageous Girl. Courageous Girls come in all shapes and sizes, but the core of who a Courageous Girl is becoming can be summed up in the following acronym:

C—Confident in who God made her to be
O—Open to those who are different from her
U—Understands and applies God's Word in daily life
R—Risks because her faith is in a big God
A—Asks for help (both in the form of personal prayer and within her community)
G—Generous with her time and resources
E—Empathetic
O—Obedient to God
U—Unique from the world around her
S—Servant-hearted

G—Good friend (even when it's hard)
I—Initiates with integrity
R—Real and honest with God and others
L—Lives and loves wholeheartedly

Finally, Courageous Girls are present. They are committed to continually shedding others' expectations, and they fight to be in the here and now. They are responsible, are fully in tune with the Spirit, and bear fruit because of their relationship with Him: "The fruit of the Spirit is love, joy, peace, patience, kindness, goodness, faithfulness, gentleness, self-control; against such things there is no law. And those who belong to Christ Jesus have crucified the flesh with its passions and desires. If we live by the Spirit, let us also keep in step with the Spirit. Let us not become conceited, provoking one another, envying one another" (Gal. 5:22–26 ESV).

Paul spent many of his epistles urging both Jews and Greeks to live with freedom so that they would not be overcome by the sin, strife, and immaturity rampant in their cultures. The church of Corinth had been succumbed to strong sociocultural influences, and the church of Galatia was caught up in legalistic rules and doctrines adhered to prior to Christ. Sound familiar? Being a Courageous Girl is not for the faint of heart but for those who desire to be like Lucia: uninhibited by dots *or* stars—totally free. It is difficult to live as if we are truly loved. It is even harder to teach others to do this. It is a muscle that must be strengthened through practice and developed in our children in ordinary moments as we act out of the abundance of love we have received.

The following chapters unveil practical steps and activities for both you and your daughter to live as if you are loved so that you both can embrace courage. If practiced, they will help you create space for slow and steady shifts in your relationship. Spend a little time each day cultivating these important action steps, and consider discussing noticeable changes with other moms as you choose to live courageously.

Takeaway

Make a list of five attributes you notice and adore in your daughter and five attributes you notice and appreciate about yourself. Try to keep your list focused on your God-given attributes (like wisdom or attention to detail) instead of temporary traits (like good grades or athletic achievements). Once you have a list for you and a list for your daughter, pray over these traits daily. Keep them by your bedside and ask God to develop them in you and your daughter. Ask Him to use these qualities to protect you both and build your resiliency. Pray that you would both see these gifts in connection with your God-given purpose and that you both would be drawn to God's design with clarity and enthusiasm. Remember, you and your daughter are on a long journey to discover whom God made you both to be. Learning to stand tall in that design can take time.

Take It a Step Further

Ask your daughter to write down five traits that she believes God gave her on purpose. How does her list compare with your list? Talk about what each of you wrote and how she shows her gifts to her family, to her friends, and to the outside world. If you can, model this activity for your daughter. Allow yourself to be vulnerable to your daughter, and share something you believe God gave you that is helping you live out your greater purpose.

2

She Embraces Holy Crap

The Spirit of the Sovereign LORD is on me, because the LORD has anointed me to proclaim good news to the poor. He has sent me to bind up the brokenhearted, to proclaim freedom for the captives and release from darkness for the prisoners, to proclaim the year of the LORD's favor and the day of vengeance of our God, to comfort all who mourn, and provide for those who grieve in Zion—to bestow on them a crown of beauty instead of ashes, the oil of joy instead of mourning, and a garment of praise instead of a spirit of despair. They will be called oaks of righteousness, a planting of the LORD for the display of his splendor. They will rebuild the ancient ruins and restore the places long devastated; they will renew the ruined cities that have been devastated for generations.

Isaiah 61:1–4

I live several miles outside town in the quiet hills of Oregon wine country. Not so long ago, the region where I live was home to a rural farming community. Given the environment, I enjoy raising small animals with my family—dogs, cats, chickens, and so forth—so I know the smell of manure. Often while I do my chores,

God has given me fresh analogies to apply to life's less-than-fragrant moments.

Several years ago, I received an impression that life sometimes feels like a huge pile of dung. There might be better words to explain this feeling, but the sense is widely understood: none of us can escape life's difficult moments. In many cases, the term *crap* feels like an enormous understatement when describing life on earth. The realities and consequences of abuse, addiction, shame, bondage, and other brokenness can feel so heavy at times that we double over in prayer, begging they will end.

Scripture tells us that the heart is deceitful (see Jer. 17:9) and that all of us fall short of God's glory (see Rom. 3:23). All of us! The fall has affected so many aspects of our human existence. So why are we surprised when hard things happen in our lives? Why do we believe that crap falls only on our shoulders and that our lives are the only ones that stink at times?

Some Christians teach the idea that if we experience anxiety, sadness, exhaustion, depression, anger, envy, or bitterness because of life's difficulties, we do not trust God enough. I recently sat in the audience at a well-respected conference and heard one of the speakers share from the microphone that it is a "sin to feel despair." I could not disagree more. Try telling that to a mother who has lost a child to cancer or lost a marriage because of her husband's addiction to pornography. This kind of theology causes us to hide, covered by and cowering in shame, and increases our despair.

This mentality sounds a little like that of Job's friends, who asked him what he did to deserve the pain he was experiencing. According to Job 1:8, Job was "blameless—a man of complete integrity. He fear[ed] God and stay[ed] away from evil" (NLT). Job's three friends, Eliphaz, Bildad, and Zophar, tried to comfort Job with their presence after he lost everything—his family, his livelihood, and his health. In their attempt to care for Job, they told their friend that the suffering he was experiencing was his fault, and they instructed him to repent. Job responded, "You are miserable comforters, all of you!" (16:2). Too often we falsely think that the plight of our pain (or someone else's pain) or the blessings in our lives are directly correlated to God's judgment of our behavior. "What goes around comes around" is not a premise of Christianity.

I have heard this theology again and again in my office as women blame themselves for suffering in their lives. Sometimes suffering is the natural consequences of one's choices, but not always. This theology seeps into our homes when we ask our daughters what they did to provoke the bullies on the playground or blame them for the violation they experienced while under the influence at parties. We fear telling another person about our struggles because we're afraid that, rather than receiving empathy, we will be told we lack faith. The truth is, we all have struggles. It's important to recognize the smell of crap before we can acknowledge the miracle of its transformation into something holy. Life throws us unexpected curveballs, but God is still good, and meaning can still come out of the messes.

SHE BELIEVES GOD USES ANYTHING

Years ago, when diaper changes and toilet training were part of our family's daily routine, my husband and I longed for the day when *poop* was not a regularly used word in our home. The word became so entrenched in our vocabulary that God used it to give me clarity about relational and spiritual matters. In that season I pondered the purpose of poop and its role in our development as healthy people and mature disciples. My farmer friend, Beth, also known as "the egg lady" in my neck of the woods, contemplated with me the ways in which farming teaches biblical principles. As you could probably guess, poop plays a significant role in the agricultural system. Manure is highly valued by farmers who want to produce a robust harvest. It is incredibly nourishing. It turns out that the by-product from all living animals (poop) turns into a rich supply of vitamins and minerals that, when tilled into the soil, makes for stronger, thriving plants. Who knew that poop could be so essential to growth? What we consider waste in our lives and often want to get rid of, God uses to nourish us in deeper ways. The crap we experience in life either can sit useless and stink or can become some of the best nourishment for our souls.

Solomon, one of the wisest men in the Bible, boasted great riches and enjoyed all the pleasures of life. However, in Ecclesiastes he presented an ironic and unexpected truth:

> It is better to go to a house of mourning
>   than to go to a house of feasting,
> for death is the destiny of everyone;
>   the living should take this to heart.
> Frustration is better than laughter,
>   because a sad face is good for the heart.
> The heart of the wise is in the house of mourning,
>   but the heart of fools is in the house of pleasure.
> It is better to heed the rebuke of a wise person
>   than to listen to the song of fools.
> Like the crackling of thorns under the pot,
>   so is the laughter of fools.
>   This too is meaningless.
>
> Extortion turns a wise person into a fool,
>   and a bribe corrupts the heart.
>
> The end of a matter is better than its beginning,
>   and patience is better than pride. (7:2–8)

In this passage Solomon suggested that searching for wisdom and understanding in life's hardships far exceeds seeking pleasure and comfort. Death as destiny sounds gloomy, but I have seen how those who embrace mourning and acknowledge their own fragility tend to enjoy the pleasures they are given far more than those who choose to ignore the poop or try to live above life's trials. Often these wise travelers are able to move through pain by embracing the grief that comes along with it and emerge on the other side richer and more resilient. Abundant living is learning to embrace *all* of life.

I recall regular conversations with one of my dear friends, Christina. For years she and her husband longed for children but struggled with infertility. I remember our conversations about people who made insensitive comments out of naivete—easy pregnancies and multiple babies can lead one to believe that it is a simple process. People often take having a baby for granted until a ten-year journey turns the desperate effort into a job rather than a romantic endeavor. After several years of fertility treatments, in vitro fertilization miraculously brought them a child, a precious girl. For their second child, they moved forward with plans to adopt, knowing how unlikely another conception would be. However, the adoption took years longer than they imagined because of international government bureaucracy. They experienced more waiting. More disappointment. More *poop.*

They agreed to consider adopting a baby with special needs. They simply wanted to hold the child God intended them to love. As has been the case with several women I know, Christina became pregnant after bringing home their adopted daughter. This time the pregnancy occurred without any human intervention. I believe that years of infertility challenges resulted in this family placing a high and rightful value on their children, far more than most.

Each daughter is a miracle in her own right, and my friend has responded to these gifts with great, intentional parenting, such that comes only from knowing the depth of pain and sorrow that precedes blessing. She is a beautiful example of a mom who turned life's manure into something holy.

Walking alongside clients and friends through seasons of drought has shown me that no one wants to be alone in brokenness. Part of the spirit of Courageous Girls is to create community through slow, steady, trusted relationships by establishing safe spaces where authenticity and vulnerability (showing our poop) can be practiced without the risk of rejection. Three things allow this to take place: honesty, mercy, and love. This is how God works, both in and through us. Dr. Harville Hendrix said, "We are wounded in relationship, and we can be healed in relationship."[1] Honesty invites God and others to help us process and heal from our crap; it also brings awareness of how good, gracious, loving, and creative our God is. He takes poop and uses it to grow us.

As we hear the intimate details of another person's life story, there is temptation to oversimplify our responses or move through them quickly, especially if it involves pain or discomfort. Many well-intentioned mentors, friends, loved ones, and pastors can get trapped sharing biblical rhetoric that falls flat on the recipient. They might say true statements like "God has a plan" or "He will use this," but the timing of sharing those words just isn't right. Yes, the Bible offers promises we can and must cling to in turbulent waters. Jesus is most definitely our truest friend, in calm times and in the midst of any storm. However, sharing these truths in the midst of a person's raw pain must be tempered. Otherwise, it's too hard to hear and can feel minimizing, devaluing, and dismissive of one's personal story. This kind of trite response can send someone further from God rather than drawing her closer to Him.

For women who have been betrayed in their marriages and mothers who have lost children to suicide or tragic accidents, rhetoric is not enough. Their situations cannot be explained away with a verse or a well-meant poem. These stories are war stories; many of us carry them, some more quietly than others. There is really no other way to hear these stories than to sit side by side with a survivor and bear witness to her journey. As a client of mine once said, we try to put marble over dry rot with words, but they fall short. Like rich fertilizer, time and presence allow the nutrients from manure to seep deep into the ground before the fresh green blades of grass make an appearance. We must, at least for a winter season, let ourselves face the hard parts of our stories in order to look back and see how God's always-protective hand carried us through the eye of the storm.

SHE MOVES THROUGH SATURDAY: A TIME OF MOURNING

Revisiting and grieving our pain *with Jesus* and the gentle help of others is the only path to resurrection, victory, and redemption. The road map has been laid out well for us. As believers in Jesus Christ, we have established our faith on the idea that resurrection comes through suffering, death, and grief. There is no way to Sunday but through Saturday. John Ortberg explored this idea further in his devotional on despair and joy.[2] Not only did Jesus face death in all its reality, but He also remained in the tomb for three days before He rose to overcome the death sentence. His followers' devastation must have been gut wrenching: not only did their promised Messiah suffer a criminal's death, but they were also being hunted by Jesus-haters. One moment they were sitting at the feet of their Messiah, and the next moment they were living in fear and despair without any awareness that Resurrection Sunday was coming. They lived through Saturday—the day between Jesus' death and His resurrection. It was a day of unknown proportions, between the messiest of all messes (Good Friday) and pure holiness (Easter Sunday). Heavy with uncertainty, Saturday was a day of mourning.

As humans, we must mourn. We must grieve. We must learn to accept what we think is a waste and allow it to mix into the good so that it can become a part of our souls' nourishment. The tapestry of our journey is often a wad of knots that we do not want others to see. There is no point trying to keep the two extremes of our lives separate: one holy and pure, the other failures and darkness. This is where clinical practice and scientific wisdom meet the biblical truth of grace and redemption. Grieving is a skill most of us do not possess until we are forced to practice it. Even then, we often want to minimize our feelings, push them away, or mask them. A gentle reminder, sweet mama: hard hearts equal soft faith. Only through softening our hearts and feeling all the agony of grief does our faith have a chance to flourish. The true equation is this: soft hearts equal stronger faith!

Over the years, one of the most common questions I hear from clients is "How long will this take? One, two, or three sessions?" The problem with poop is that no matter how far away it flies or how well it is hidden, you can always smell it! I once heard a story from a kids' ministry leader in a nearby church who served with the three-year-olds on Sunday mornings. One Sunday morning the kids were playing in the church classroom when the teacher smelled a foul odor. She followed her nose to a corner of the room where a little boy was happily building a tower out of brightly colored blocks. The odor grew stronger. She bent down and asked the little boy whether he needed to use the bathroom. "No," he replied calmly, without looking up from his masterpiece. Just then, the teacher noticed a little pile of poop next to the boy. He had not wanted to stop his project to use the bathroom, so he left it in the corner, assuming someone else would clean up his business! Let this be a lesson to us all: if you let your poop sit unattended, not only will it turn into a bigger mess, but it will make a mess of other people's lives too. This is a humorous story, but the implications are less amusing. The hurts of life can turn us into people who hurt others or refuse to be loved, whether we mean to or not. When you willingly step toward processing your pain and grieve in healthy ways, something beautiful emerges—*you*, as God intended you to be. Courage to let go of the past allows us to open our hands and embrace what is and what could be. This takes time.

I am often asked, "What's the point of revisiting or ruminating on the pain of the past? Won't that make my experience worse?" This question comes frequently from the teachers, police officers, pastors, counselors, nurses, and physicians who sit in my office. Interestingly, they are some of the bravest in our community. They live to help others, but when it comes to their own stories, they give themselves little permission to heal. Many of these people are so successful in their careers because they are exceptional at dissociating, a term used in the clinical world to describe when a person separates himself or herself from a stressful or traumatic event in order to survive it. Like traveling a regular route home and not remembering you stopped at a stop sign or red light, dissociation is a way to coast through life without being emotionally present. God created dissociation as a means to help us cope in the most horrific of moments, but the brain will not shut down this coping strategy until we have confirmed the safety of ourselves or others. When people have experienced trauma, they learn to sail through life above the waves so that they are not caught in the undertow of emotions lying in the depth of their souls. But remember, the waves and wind are often the very things that can bring us closer to God. Isaiah 61 reminds us that this is why Jesus came: to heal the brokenhearted and to bring comfort to those who mourn (see vv. 1–2).

Think about it: if we are totally honest, we're all pretty good at dissociating. New mothers tend to their infants day and night, even after lengthy and challenging births, despite functioning on extremely low levels of rest. This trauma affects a mother's body, yet each day she does it again. Community helpers and leaders take care of others because they have a high tolerance for trauma. The problem is that dissociating never allows for resolution, which means that a person's body, brain, and soul are continually processing pain that eventually and inadvertently leaks into other parts of life. What parts of your history have been sealed shut or are not permitted to surface? What stories or lies do you carry deep inside that catch you off guard? These are the experiences that need to be faced; we must grieve the losses so that we will be able to have compassion for others. Dismissing our own pain leads to dismissing the pain of our loved ones around us. The illusion of skipping Saturday and jumping miraculously from Friday to Sunday is not only unhealthy but may actually signal unresolved trauma. Modeling to our daughters that a Courageous Girl accepts mourning as a necessary part of emotional health reveals the ways God renews devastated places (see Isa. 61:4).

SHE WAITS FOR SUNDAY: A TIME OF REJOICING

Saturday was a day of grieving, but then Sunday came—and with it, the resurrection and restoration promised. Imagine being one of the disciples at the time of Jesus' death. After such despair on Saturday, the empty tomb turned their mourning into rejoicing. Death could not hold Him down. In the darkness of our mess, when Resurrection

Sunday feels too far away, we still hold on to the promises of paradise, where there is no more sin, no more tears, and no more death (Rev. 21:4, 27). In moments of confusion and guttural sorrow, I long for heaven.

While raising daughters in a world full of crap, we can cling to the hope of heaven. We must hold on to God's greater story and teach it to our girls. I've pored over the pages of my well-worn Bible, looking for God's exact play-by-play. How do I protect my daughters' hearts from the inevitable pain of this life? How do I get us around Saturday and make it to Sunday? Friends, we cannot get to Sunday on our own. Our grief, loss, regret, and pain will hold us in Saturday until we give them back to the One who can redeem and repurpose them. Jesus is who He says He is—the one who came for the sick and sinner, not the well. He is the only professed Messiah in history who actually rose from the dead and conquered death. He is the only one whose nails pinned sin to the cross. He is the only one who can take all the crap in our lives and somehow make it holy. This far exceeds our abilities. Though we may try to heal our hurt or the hurt of others, that is not our job. We can never accomplish this on our own. We will never think or feel or cry our way to healing. Our hope must rest in Him alone.

God is in the business of transforming death and hopelessness into resurrected life and new beginnings. Isaiah 61 says we will receive a double share in the place of shame (see v. 7). Our daughters desperately need to understand this in the core of their beings. They need to watch us experience this kind of powerful transformation as we work through our own grief and pain with Jesus. So often we let our daughters see only the resolved version of ourselves, but they never get to witness our growth process. This is critical to their ability to recognize and normalize their own humanity. They will see the difference in us when our hearts have been healed; they will feel the peace that exists when our souls are finally at rest.

Let's surround ourselves with those who are honest and real—those who surrender the masks of measuring up in exchange for the authenticity of grace and forgiveness. Let's become these women and walk alongside others in this journey. In the words of Francesca Battistelli in one of my favorite songs, "Mercy's waiting on the other side / If we're honest."[3]

SHE IS HONEST

One of the greatest gifts of having a Courageous Girls group is an intentional safe space where moms help one another consistently work through the crap in their lives. This space is grace, because it's the extension of undeserved favor given again and again. Part of this process involves casting out fears of the unknown, fears that we naturally feel as mothers and as women. These fears can be driven by sensationalized media and worldviews that suggest we have no authority over our children and no basis to hope for a better future. The fears can come from our own life experiences that have taught us that we are powerless and unheard. This lie was already defeated by Jesus. The truth is that we can absolutely influence our daughters' lives by being connected and maintaining strong, meaningful relationships with them. By freeing ourselves from paralyzing fear, we can keep our trauma from leaking into our daughters' lives while we help them navigate paradigms differently. We can do this because of Jesus' love and power in and through us. Let's invite God to work in us and cast out the fear with which we wrestle. Let's live out new paradigms with our children and teach them to do the same. When our daughters practice honesty with us, may we handle their vulnerability with great care and show them that honesty breeds wholeness.

SHE HAS GRACE

Does it ever seem as if the house never truly gets clean? Or once you clean it up, it becomes messy again? Have you gardened before and recognized that the weeds always return? *What's the deal?* One of the lies we have accepted is that the more mature we become in Christ, the less crap one has. I don't know about you, but it doesn't make logical sense to me. I think that if we asked Farmer Beth about her livestock, she would say that as long as her animals are living, they are producing manure. As all mamas know, our children never stop pooping. I think maturing in Christ and becoming healthy, courageous women is more about knowing what to do with our poop than it is about not having any.

My husband built me the most beautiful chicken lodge I could imagine. And while it's wonderful to have farm-fresh eggs in the morning, there is always more chicken poop than there are eggs. Being human means that my sin, my pain, my brokenness, and my struggles are all God's to use for His purposes. I see it daily. But just as chicken waste becomes highly valuable fertilizer once it has been processed, our brokenness can be transformed to nourish the soul. Maybe the message that we should promulgate—and that aligns more with gospel-centered truth—is that Jesus is in the business of resurrecting, returning, and repurposing what the enemy has tried to kill, steal, and destroy (see John 10:10).

One of the Courageous Girls groups I lead has been extremely challenging and messy. These groups are not free of issues, but that's the point. Right now we are battling hard things like mean-girl behaviors and a lack of healthy communication habits (even within the group) that will help these women guide and coach their daughters toward healthier relationships. We are all in process, and it is our job to coach our girls. The pain of being human continues to sting. Yet I am convinced that this kind of environment is critical; we need to practice being less judgmental about who we are or are not and who others are or are not. The reality is that we are all made up of the potential for good and bad. Genesis 1:27 teaches that males and females were made in God's image and that we are a beautiful reflection of the glorious ways of God. However, when we are given free will, it seems we often choose a path of destruction. We become discontent, curious, strong willed, and prideful. Dealing with the consequences of the choices we make and the behaviors we embrace, particularly in family and community, is difficult.

Teaching our daughters how to be honest about their thoughts, emotions, behaviors, and needs happens in a safe environment with a sturdy foundation where pain can be used for character-building and maturing. Safety is felt when we know that we can show all of ourselves without being judged, defined, or forced to pretend. It is solidified when we sit and process together. The first step in building a safe relationship with our daughters is to be honest as moms and to allow our daughters to be honest with us. A foundation of trust is built, and they will come to us again. When they feel they can tell us anything without being met with immediate judgment, criticism, withheld love, or hijacking our emotions, they will grow up to know what grace looks and feels like with God and others.

This does not mean that our job is to be totally permissive parents who never discipline our children or give consequences. What this means is that—*first*—we listen to their hearts. We don't react immediately. We are slow to speak, quick to listen (see James 1:19). We do not rush to judgments or assumptions. We do not worry about how our children's actions will reflect on us or how others perceive us. We listen and create space where they can be heard, and we get them the help they need. We regulate our emotions. This practice is intentional and requires great awareness on our part, but it reflects God's character in the flesh. And when we blow it, we own it and make it right. Play-therapy expert Dr. Landreth and others said it this way: "What's most important may not be what you do, but what you do after what you did!"[4] Our faith is founded on repentance and forgiveness. Life from death. Beauty out of ashes. Grace is the only way.

SHE RECEIVES GRACE

When my youngest daughter was five, she confessed that she had been hiding my husband's most treasured cookies, the Christmas spritz. Jeff's mom gives him bags full of spritz cookies every Christmas, and Jeff hides them in the freezer to last throughout the winter nights. Covered in spritz cookie crumbs and greasy fingerprints, Nevie was honest about a bag we found in her closet. My gluten-free daughter was hoarding food in her bedroom, hiding it from the rest of the family, but I was still a proud mama—not because of the dishonest act but because of the courage she demonstrated in confessing what she had done. It was an indication that she was growing up in a home where she felt safe and secure, so much so that she was willing to unearth her secret in order to heal the places inside her heart that had been torn up by keeping it. Most kids have similar consciences. They desire to be honest and to please their parents. They also desire to be known for who they truly are. Don't we all?

Nevie and I talked about how good it felt to confess her secret and to be seen in full light. I was tempted, naturally, to discipline her for stealing and lying and all the other wrong behaviors I could identify. However, because of God's grace and my play-therapy training, I was able to see past the behavior (thank You, Jesus) and allow God to use this opportunity to develop rich soil. I held my tongue and instead listened and reflected back her own conclusions about why she had done that and how it had made her heart feel. I affirmed Nevie's choice to trust me and divulge the secret; in doing so, something that the enemy would have used to twist my daughter's sense of confidence and integrity was instead used to nourish the soil of her heart.

As our Courageous Girls group tackles middle school, we rely on the years of relationship we have built with one another and with Jesus. We have developed the kind of intimacy that grows only over long periods of time spent with Jesus and loving one another through the good, the bad, and the smelly. We have had hard, uncomfortable conversations over the years but have emerged on the other side intact. This is why Courageous Girls groups need to be long term. One year is not enough to see the depths of one another or to traverse difficult situations without losing faith in one another's humanity. I want our daughters to know that no matter what they do or what has been done to them, God can use it all to make something beautiful! Embracing the holy crap in all our lives is how we remind ourselves that we are all experiencing the ongoing process of sanctification. Surrendering to Jesus is a learning process and requires a community in which we can learn and grow. Accepting that poop has a place and potential in God's economy reveals the strength and humility of a Courageous Girl.

Takeaway

What poop have you buried from your past? Revisit a past hurt or struggle for a moment. How did you overcome that? If there is still work to be done, make a commitment to find resources to help you: a local support group, a counselor, a trusted accountability partner, a good friend who has experienced something similar. Remember that being honest with yourself and another about the pain it caused is the first step in healing.

Take It a Step Further

Don't stop there. Get gut-wrenchingly real with yourself. How has your past hurt and pain seeped into your family's life? Specifically, how is it affecting your daughter? Is she showing signs of similar struggles or facing challenges that trigger your own past? What are you willing to start addressing today? If you are unsure, read through Isaiah 61 and pay attention to the words and phrases that stand out to you. Notice how God's greater redemption plan is moving from loss to restoration. Waiting for heaven or just hoping your daughter figures it out on her own is not enough. Ask God to guide you in helping your daughter become a mighty oak, rooted in God's Word and healing. Write these thoughts, emotions, and hopes in your journal so that, later in your life, you will remember what God has done.

3

She Feels to Heal

*There are few more viscerally transformational experiences
than the secure embrace of a loving parent, especially
when the child truly recognizes their need.*
Jay Wolf, *Hope Heals*

*Praise be to the God and Father of our Lord Jesus Christ, the
Father of compassion and the God of all comfort, who comforts
us in all our troubles, so that we can comfort those in any
trouble with the comfort we ourselves receive from God.*
2 Corinthians 1:3–4

I was twenty-five by the time I could acknowledge I had feelings.
I recall my closest girlfriends confronting me in college for being
overly optimistic. I was confused; I thought being positive was a
godly attribute. I had only practiced "mind over matter" and chosen
to find the silver lining in every situation. My parents instilled in
me an ability to reframe my circumstances, a powerful skill I will
discuss in later chapters. However, I did not know how to process

negative emotions well. I viewed vulnerable emotions as excuses, signs of weakness, and obstacles to living the fullest life. Most of my mentors in the church had reinforced this perspective and affirmed my outlook in unintentional ways. However, as I ventured through my training as a clinician, I learned how failing to model healthy processing of negative feelings can cause children to cope in potentially damaging ways.

I learned to cope with negative emotions through an eating disorder called bulimia. As a curvy young girl growing up in a culture that idealized a thin frame, I did not let anyone know about my unpleasant feelings, like disappointment, insecurity, loneliness, and discouragement. Instead of directly acknowledging and naming those feelings, I tried to relieve those emotions by controlling my body size. Like most parents, we follow the generational patterns of our family line unless we consciously choose to learn a different way. My parents made huge efforts to shift the legacy of their homes, and I am grateful for the ways I was able to navigate my struggles over time.

SHE EMBRACES THE RAINBOW OF EMOTIONS

Regardless of our stories, if we do not address negative emotions with our children, we open their lives to a plethora of unhealthy coping mechanisms. Maladaptive behaviors related to controlling emotions include food restriction, weight tracking, overeating, bingeing, and compulsive exercising, and more pain-numbing behaviors like drinking, smoking, vaping, drug use, pornography use, sex, masturbation, self-harm, and a myriad of other challenges. Learning how to process every emotion that a girl feels is part of the journey of becoming courageous.

The United States is ranked as one of the world's most addicted and desensitized societies.[1] This reality, coupled with our culture's current state of numbing activities (acting on the desire to check out from reality), is not encouraging. There is little to inspire hope that things will improve across our nation. One of the reasons for this is that we do not have a cultural norm for grieving. We are not expected to move healthily through our God-designed emotions; we prefer fast-food–type processing that makes us happy. We teach kids to "toughen up" or to "grin and bear it." We are coached to "fake it till we make it" and to "play through the pain." In church circles we can even succumb to the idea that negative emotions are ungodly and train ourselves to focus on the blessings. I have heard these phrases taught to both boys and girls, though girls are hardwired with higher sensitivity to their environment and relational dynamics than boys. This fascinating difference in brain development is another reason why our daughters need help honoring their emotions.[2]

SHE RECOGNIZES DENIAL

Growing up, I viewed myself as a good girl, so I hid my internal conflict. Rather than showing my struggles through risky external behaviors like drinking or releasing emotional tension through sex or angry outbursts, I disconnected from my true heart and focused on performing well in school, sports, leadership, and body-image management. Since I was not processing with anyone outside my own head, I developed many false narratives that I held deep inside. I know many girls can relate. I also know my parents never meant to teach me that it was wrong to express feelings; my family has discussed this openly in my adult years. However, we all have a tendency, especially in Christian circles, to ignore our feelings and push past them.

Our tendency to ignore our negative emotions might stem from our families' habits, or we might have practiced denial for so long that it feels normal. Some cultures suppress emotions more than others. Asian cultures are notorious for this tendency and leave individuals at high risk for developing unhealthy habits around emotional intelligence. Regardless of the ways we suppress emotions, all dysfunctional families convey, intentionally or unintentionally, these basic rules: (1) do not talk about anything meaningful, (2) do not trust others, and (3) do not allow yourself to feel your emotions. We transmit most of these lessons indirectly through patterns lived out in our ordinary daily lives.[3]

Our children catch what we live, not necessarily what we say. For example, when they hear a mom lying to a friend about why she cannot attend a gathering, this models that bending the truth is a clever way to avoid conflict. Or a home without any conflict conveys that it's inappropriate to discuss feelings. Think about the wife who never tells her husband that he hurt her feelings. Imagine he scolded her for overextending her budget at the grocery store, but instead of communicating her hurt, she just turns to the dishes at the kitchen sink so that no one sees the tears silently streaming down her cheeks. The child living in this home may know her father acted unkindly but never learns from her mother how to handle his belittling behavior. If the mother suffers in silence and promptly becomes cheery at the next opportunity to transition out of her sadness, the moment is gone and so are the emotions that came with it.

Another common practice of denial is parents teaching children not to tell "family secrets." Children are programmed not to trust anyone outside their family (despite dishonesty within the family) and to avoid sharing what may happen within the walls of the home. Not wanting to ruffle feathers or be seen as ungrateful, children alter how they might otherwise act, especially how they express themselves.

These messages, embedded in young, impressionable brains, create deep neural pathways that affect children's development. Do these messages sound familiar to you? Can you identify any messages from the dysfunctional family system?

SHE REGULATES HER EMOTIONS

If you have received messages from a dysfunctional family system that practices denial, it's important to know that we can retrain ourselves to recognize and regulate our emotions. Even if we have grown up with a distorted view of negative emotions, we can learn to pay attention to what they tell us about our reality. For example, when we feel angry, we might notice that our jaws tighten or our hands start to clench. This kind of body awareness helps people learn their natural responses to the world around them. Sometimes children have a stomachache when they are anxious. When we can identify the emotions, we can help them calm down. This is called *self-regulating*, a term that counselors use to describe how to be aware of one's feelings and meet a human need in a legitimate way. If I could pinpoint the one skill that I have needed to teach in my counseling practice more than any other skill, it would be the ability to self-regulate. Before I explain how to develop this strength, I want to explain why *feeling* is so important.

Healthy brain development and spiritual formation require that we learn to process our feelings, especially when those feelings are more intense. A myth, inadvertently taught by Christian families, is that faith is primarily related to what we *think* to be true. This rationale places primary importance on the frontal lobe (upper brain), which is responsible for decision-making and rational thoughts. This assumption undermines the way God created humans and the importance of the amygdala (lower brain), which plays a central role in our experience of emotions. Often this form of mind over matter stresses that we must not "give in to our emotions." This teaching comes from passages like Romans 12:2, "the renewing of your mind," and 2 Corinthians 10:5, "We take captive every thought to make it obedient to Christ." Undoubtedly, these are powerful Scriptures, and we will address them in a later chapter. However, framing faith as a primarily thought-based exercise causes us to cast our emotions in a negative light. Ultimately this causes us to compartmentalize our lives and prevents us from fully integrating all of who we are. The Lord wants *all* of us: mind, heart, body, and actions. That includes our emotions. There are thirty-nine verses throughout the Bible that speak to loving God with our whole hearts. There are many more verses that encourage us to love God with *all* of who we are.

One of the most well-known verses says, "Love the Lord your God with all your heart and with all your soul and with all your strength and with all your mind" (Luke 10:27). When we experience disconnect between our minds, bodies, and emotions, we need to pause and assess what's happening. When I was a new mom, I lost my workout routine (for a good cause). However, without a way to regularly release stress, my irritation was flaring and my anxiety was rising. My body knew I would feel better if I could exercise a few times each week, but my mind kept telling me that I was a bad mom if I took time away from my daughters. My mind also told me that my lack of exercise was Jeff's fault because … well, there was no real reason, but I just needed someone to blame.

Taking time to pause and reflect, I listened to what was happening inside my body (anxiety), my emotions (irritation and bitterness), and my mind (a workout would help me, but good moms do not take time away from their babies to exercise). Doing so helped me work through the three warring parts of myself before the Lord. I decided to comfort my body and emotions by making an exercise plan. My mind soon learned that Jeff was not standing in my way, and my babies did fine without me for three hours a week. In fact, I was a better mom when I was with them because of my regular exercise. It is not healthy to lead only with our emotions, nor is it healthy to lead only with our logic. Loving God with all of who we are requires integrating our emotions with our minds and our bodies. So how do we move in this direction?

Dr. Daniel Siegel, a leading neuropsychiatrist, and parenting expert Tina Payne Bryson, PhD, have helped the mental-health field understand how a person develops healthy decision-making, self-awareness, school success, relationships, and other important aspects that lead one to wellness and integration. They use a clever analogy of a two-story house, describing a child's brain as having both an upstairs and a downstairs. The downstairs brain, responsible for the lower-level functioning, is in charge of impulses, emotions, and basic life functions like breathing and blinking. The upstairs brain is responsible for mental processing—decision-making, morality, empathy, and self-awareness. The upstairs brain is constantly under construction until a person reaches his or her midtwenties (did you catch that?); the downstairs brain is fully functional at birth.[4] Pause for a moment and let that sink in. Our children need a lot of patience and coaching throughout their growing years. If we were not coached in our childhood, we might need them too!

If we consider the brain, we see that from the beginning God created us as emotional beings—with basic functionality—who are primarily sensory oriented. He did not give us the ability to fully engage our logical brains until the middle of our twenties, well into adulthood. This explains why I wasn't fully able to articulate my own emotions until age twenty-five. A significant part of our jobs as parents is to support our children's emotional brain development by helping them put vocabulary words to their feelings. Without help, we are left to navigate our inner worlds alone, and we do not have the full capacity to reason until we become adults. Some of the conclusions we make in our emotional brains are not based on facts but only on our sensory perceptions. Authors Milan and Kay Yerkovich wrote, "When a parent listens to us and asks questions, we have an opportunity to reflect and put words to what's going on inside us. The self-awareness that comes from learning to reflect gives us the ability to understand our reactions, behaviors, needs, and inner conflicts when we're adults."[5] As parents, we are the helpers who integrate the two halves (emotional and relational) of our children's brains so that they can develop into whole and relationally healthy adults.

It is mind blowing to realize that God designed us to map out our world through emotional attachments. Before we can make cognitive sense of our worlds with our fully developed frontal lobes, we are still drawing conclusions about our world from a gut level. God so graciously designed us in a way that we need our parents (and others) in order to develop secure connections and become whole beings. This is why we in Courageous Girls focus so much on emotional health and attunement (the ability to sense natural emotional rhythms, patterns, and connections within ourselves and others). We are able to "love because he first loved us" (1 John 4:19). Our children will not be able to love others well unless they first experience what it is like to be loved completely, big emotions and all!

Self-regulation occurs when we do something to calm ourselves down, such as go for a walk, breathe deeply, journal, listen to music, or exercise. As Dr. Siegel said, the most emotionally healthy people are those who know how to keep both their upstairs and downstairs engaged.[6] This does not come naturally but must be taught to our girls and modeled by us moms. Those who grew up in chaotic, emotionally neglectful, narcissistic, or abusive homes find self-regulating harder than most. The necessity of mapping out danger has given our brains a fast track to protect and react before assessing safety. God created this automatic system to help us in danger; without it, we would be far more vulnerable in crisis. For example, this warning system helps a person to quickly slam on his or her car brakes when approaching the red brake lights from an abruptly slowing car in front. This system is extremely helpful in the midst of real danger but damaging when it goes off too frequently or at unnecessary times.

Learning to self-regulate our emotional brains takes a lot of practice, safety, patience, and self-awareness, especially if we have been accustomed to ignoring our bodies and feelings over many years. Here's a helpful process to walk you through the steps of being more emotionally aware as a mom:

1. Identify the emotion. (Name it as accurately as you can.)
2. Identify where the emotion is in the body (where are you feeling changes in your body?) and where the emotion registers on your emotional thermometer (on a scale of zero to ten, with ten being the most intense).
3. Identify the source, if possible. (What caused it?)
4. Identify what that particular emotion needs. (What would bring comfort or calm it down?)
5. Advocate for that need. (This can be a hard one to learn, but practice helps.)

I usually ask the following questions in a prayerful manner, and I encourage you to try the same before teaching your daughters to regulate their emotions. It might look something like this:

Lord, I am feeling something negative after Bible study. What is that feeling?
Vulnerability.

Lord, where do I feel vulnerable in my body?
It's your gut. It feels restless, like churning.

What would You say is the source of it, Lord?
You want to be liked, and you didn't get any feedback from the group.

What does that vulnerability need?
You need someone to remind you that you are still loved and liked. You need to know that I still used what you were able to give today.

Where do I turn for that affirmation, Lord?
I can give that to you. You are always enough to Me, Terra. You can also ask someone from your encouragement team to remind you of who you are.

My prayerful reflection usually ends like this:
Lord, help me have courage to advocate for my needs and move into action. Show me again how You designed me and made me precious to You.

I might text a friend for encouragement or wait for the Lord to send some my way.
The result: usually peace. Sometimes it takes time.

Vulnerability is not my favorite emotion. (Can you tell?) You know the feeling: the one that creeps in right after you share an embarrassing story or try to offer wisdom in a room full of people you do not know well. You wonder what they think of you as they stare at you awkwardly with distant smiles. The truth is, you will never know what they really think. It feels like walking through town after forgetting to put on your clothes. I still dread that feeling, yet I try to practice what I preach.

The most powerful teaching moments are the ones full of raw and real emotions—emotions we'd like to cover up with a gentle sniffle and polite smile but that really come out as heaving sobs and constant nasal drip. When we honor how we actually feel (versus how we *think* we should feel or *wish* we felt) and teach our daughters to do the same, we teach them that they matter. We impart to them a tangible truth that God meets them where they are and that they are important and worthy of our attention, care, and concern. Every person wants to know she is the apple of someone's eye. Walking your daughter through this exact process after a particularly challenging day at school or after a disappointing loss will help her identify her emotions and grow her own emotional awareness, and it will draw you closer together as she builds greater trust in your relationship.

I love King David and his psalms; they are full of passion, deep emotions, and raw humanity. You can actually see David processing his emotions through songwriting, journaling, and prayer. In Psalm 17:6–9, David wrote, "I call on you, my God, for you will answer me; turn your ear to me and hear my prayer. Show me the wonders of your great love, you who save by your right hand those who take refuge in you from their foes. Keep me as the apple of your eye; hide me in the shadow of your wings from the wicked who are out to destroy me, from my mortal enemies who surround me."

You can hear the desperation in his cry as Saul and his army hunted for him. In his plea I hear that David deeply trusted that God would answer his cry and turn toward him. Not only did David know God would hear him, but he also believed God would show him great demonstrations of love so that David could find refuge in Him. King David is a wonderful example of a person after God's heart, yet he felt an extremely wide range of emotions.

SHE CAN IDENTIFY HER OWN FEELINGS AND CONNECT WITH THE EMOTIONS OF OTHERS

As I mentioned earlier, I once heard a leader preach from the pulpit that it is a sin to feel despair. This person believed that true faith in God means we should never be anxious or experience sadness because we should always find joy in all that we do. I am unconvinced this is biblical. In fact, I think there are so many verses around emotional regulation because God knows we have emotions and expects us to experience them. Being happy all the time, speeding through the concourse of life on the autopilot of joy, does not reflect the full image of God. God displays an array of emotions in Scripture. We talk about the Bible telling us to "be content in all circumstances," but that comes from Paul speaking of how he learned to be content in all circumstances (see Phil. 4:11)—a declaration, not a commandment. In other words, "Do not be anxious about anything, but in ... prayer and petition" (Phil. 4:6) is a guide for when we *are* anxious, not a rebuke for experiencing anxiety. God isn't wagging His finger and with a stern brow saying, "Do not ...," but rather He is saying, "Oh, honey, don't be anxious, for I am here."

When Lazarus died, Jesus wept with Mary and Martha (see John 11:35). Jesus knew that He would soon raise Lazarus from the dead, but He joined these beloved women in pain even though He knew healing was coming. This is what I want to exemplify for my daughters. If we can be Courageous Mamas who join our girls wherever they are on their emotional thermometers (even when we know the situation is not as critical as they may believe it is in the moment), they will have healthier brain development overall. This is empathy: the ability to see and feel someone else's experience whether you have experienced it or not. Girls will grow up to be healthier adults with a better chance at having healthier emotional relationships. Their memories will be more intact, and their brains will store them with more clarity. And best of all, our daughters will have a greater chance of understanding and embodying the kind of love our God has and offers us.

When my youngest daughter was a baby, she would nuzzle her nose into my armpit and sleep with her face surrounded by my arms. She was hiding in the shadow of my wings, finding rest and comfort. I want to live like this with God, and I want to teach my girls how to do the same. The process of teaching our daughters how to find refuge in times of anxiety, disappointment, anger, jealousy, and other difficult emotions is a journey fostered by intentionally pursuing their hearts. The greatest chance for our girls to believe God meets them in real life is for them to experience that reality with those whom they trust the most: their moms. A Courageous Girl can name her emotions, she can identify and advocate for her needs, and she can find comforting peace in her relationship with God and other trusted people in her life.

Part of teaching our children empathy is paying attention to teaching moments when they arise. Unfortunately, it is easy to indirectly communicate to our kids that they do not matter by ignoring or minimizing their emotions. This approach affects their ability to identify their emotions accurately and to empathize with others. We all do this, intentionally or otherwise, and as a trained professional counselor, I am no different. For example, if your daughter falls and bumps her knee, you might tell her to "be a big girl" or to "laugh it off." If you tell her "You are fine" or ignore her to mitigate her "drama queen tendencies," you also invalidate her experience. When your daughter says she does not want to go to school, you may say, "You don't have a choice" or "You have a pretty good life if the worst thing you have to do is go to school." When you tell her to "suck it up," you communicate that her problems do not matter.

A more subtle but equally dangerous response is when our children's pain evokes powerful emotions in us. If your daughter tells you that a friend said something mean to her, you may respond with your own hurt emotions. Your own outrage (how dare someone treat your daughter that way!) might provoke you to get mad at the friend too. In this situation your daughter must comfort you or minimize her pain in order to protect you. Instead of you leaning in to your daughter's emotional need, your emotions hijack the conversation and your anger becomes the focus. This is not empathy, though it may feel like it. An inability to regulate our emotions when our children are in pain communicates we cannot handle what they feel. The indirect message is *Your emotions are too big for me! Therefore, you are on your own.* In essence, we tell our children to suppress their feelings since we are not ready, capable, or willing to address their emotions with them. Because parents are children's first depiction of who God is, our actions can convey that God is not strong enough to handle our feelings. When this is communicated, children learn to hold back their emotions from their families and from God.

These are all things that relatively healthy parents do; there is no shame in admitting to these moments. I know how deeply these actions affect my kids, and even I still do it! Therein lies our need for grace. As moms, we cannot hear this word enough. We *must* extend grace, to ourselves and to our girls growing in their own courage and strength. Our daughters are looking to us to teach them how to move through and regulate emotions, not how to move around and avoid them.

SHE LISTENS WELL

One of the easiest ways to practice grace with our children is to grow in the discipline of listening. Learning to empathize with our daughters not only helps them calm their brains and build trust but also teaches them how to empathize with others. We cannot give away what we have not received. There are lots of ways experts teach how to listen well. For the sake of simplicity, here are three effective and essential ingredients to being a good listener: mirroring, validating, and empathizing.

Mirroring is reflecting back what a person is saying. This is not a time for interpretation, and questions should not be asked until the person is completely done sharing. Questions can often dominate and control a conversation and will shut down the other person before we hear the whole story. Clarifying questions can be asked after the speaker has shared all she wants to share. This might determine what questions you actually ask in the end. Mirroring might look like this:

Addie: "Mom, I was frustrated and embarrassed today when you said I hadn't cleaned my room in front of my friend."

Me (in an authentic and caring tone): "It did not feel good to you when I pointed out that you did not clean your room in front of your friend."

Addie: "Yes! Exactly."

Me: "Are you finished, or do you have more to share with me?"

Addie: "No, that is it."

Me: "Can I ask a clarifying question now?"

Addie: "Sure."

Me: "What would you suggest I do differently next time?"

Addie: "It would have been nice if you waited until after we got home, when it was just us, to tell me about my room."

The benefit of mirroring is that we are able to slow our reaction by listening before we respond. In doing so, we are more likely to hear exactly what the speaker is saying. When we listen to others, we often form responses in our minds while they are still talking and miss what they are saying. When this happens, we are not truly listening. We may hear only a few words because we are more focused on our rebuttal. This approach makes us more likely to respond defensively, with incomplete information or insufficient understanding. When our children speak, it is imperative that we are present and fully focused. We need to hear our daughters' experiences in their entirety so that we, as the more experienced adults, can pay attention to their nonverbal communication—body language, tone of voice, heavy sighs, avoidance of eye contact, etc. These details can give us strong clues about our children's emotional state.

Finally, we understand the importance of mirroring from a neurological perspective. The Creator designed our brains in a magnificent way. Did you know that the part of the brain that processes auditory input is separate from the part that processes verbal output? In other words, we hear from a different part of the brain than we speak from. Our daughters process their words differently by hearing those same words repeated back to them. So often we think we are communicating clearly until we hear our words repeated back to us. When your daughter says, "No, that is not what I mean!" you can simply keep mirroring until she recognizes the message she is trying to get across. A powerful result is that the speaker, in this case your daughter, will feel her body start to calm down, and she will make better sense of her own world. Mirroring helps a girl learn what she thinks and feels and how to articulate that to those around her—a vital relational skill for every area of life.

Validating occurs when we put on someone else's lens and cognitively understand that person's perspective. Validating does not require agreement and often takes humility to be able to see someone else's viewpoint. Validating is a nonjudgmental approach that meets a person where she is. It's a crucial ingredient in learning to listen well, especially when we might be tempted to think that the other person (our child, perhaps) has an inaccurate or incomplete perspective. Validation is a way of showing respect and acknowledging that another's point of view is valid *to that person*. It's also a way to recognize that "if I was in her shoes, I might come to the same conclusion she reached." Here is an example of a response to the conversation outlined above that does *not* validate my daughter's feelings:

Addie: "It would have been nice if you waited until after we got home, when it was just us, to tell me about my room."

Me: "Well, if you hadn't waited for six days to clean your room, we wouldn't have had the discussion at all!"

Not only does a response like this invalidate Addie by refusing to see her perspective at all, but it also places her in the shadow of shame by pointing out to what degree she failed. It's like rubbing salt in an already-open wound. Most of us do not respond well to invalidation (this is true for all humans), yet we do not recognize when we are invalidating others. We often invalidate others repeatedly, especially in our own homes.

Let's look at how I could have responded to Addie in a more validating way:

Addie: "It would have been nice if you waited until after we got home, when it was just us, to tell me about my room."

Me: "I can see how you might have felt embarrassed and why you would have wanted me to wait to talk to you. It sounds like you are not upset that I talked to you about your messy room but that I did it in front of your friend. That makes a lot of sense. I didn't need to do that. There was plenty of time after we dropped your friend off to discuss the issue."

Empathizing is the final—and often missed—step in effective listening. It is less about cerebral understanding and more about emotion. This is where human attachment, connection, and comfort grow, because in empathy we receive the message "I am not alone." Empathizing looks like this:

Me: "Addie, it seems you feel frustrated, embarrassed, and maybe even disappointed that I would say this in front of your friend. Is that true?"

Addie: She nods, and I can see her shoulders relax in relief.

Giving your daughter a chance to reply and tell you more is always a good thing. In fact, you might guess the wrong emotions, and in grace, she can tell you what her feelings actually are. The point is to join her where she is and not to expect her to understand or possess an adult perspective. If a lesson needs to be learned, you can ask your daughter *after* she has been fully heard: "Are you willing to hear where I was coming from?" She might say no, and you can respect that but say, "I will give you thirty minutes, and then we can talk." Most likely if you heard her well, she will be more open to hearing you.

Empathizing with our daughters teaches them how to receive and offer empathy. This requires lots of coaching, but through trial and error, you will both improve at this skill. In time, it will serve you well in all your relationships. Neuroscientists have mapped the brain when a person is feeling empathy; there is increased blood flow throughout various regions of the brain, which creates a calming effect. Ultimately, this de-escalates strong emotions and prevents them from rising even higher on the ten-point scale so that we can engage our world with both the upstairs and the downstairs brains.

Both moms and daughters may find themselves needing these tools. Whether you are in need of them now or find yourself desperate for ways to connect with your daughter, active and effective listening is a practical and easy place to start. The end of the day or bedtime can provide for some space to listen. Slow down and take the opportunity in typical day-to-day moments to be present enough to be attuned to your daughter's feelings. Comfort is a God-designed human need. When we teach our children how to be comforted and how to offer comfort to others, we are preparing them to know how to move through the difficult pain that lurks outside the safety of our homes. By experiencing healthy relationships in our homes, our daughters have a better chance of choosing healthier relationships as teens and adults. They will also become safe places where others can land. The goal is to give our daughters lots of practice while they are young—choosing to be honest, talking about their feelings, asking for what they need, and responding appropriately when there is a negative response. In turn, we develop healthier brains in our girls and in ourselves! God is so clever.

SHE IS INTENTIONAL AND COMFORTS

One of the gifts of gathering together as Courageous Girls groups is having the regular routine of turning toward, talking to, and listening to our daughters at least once a month. That may sound absurd (aren't we listening to them all the time?), but practicing authentic communication that actively stimulates heart connection and increases emotional regulation is different from the daily rantings and rundowns. It requires intentionality and a desire to sit in her reality with her. This can be hard with the ever-increasing pace of life we all keep. It is even less likely to happen if we are constantly being drawn away by the ding of an incoming text message or the whistle of a Facebook message. But intentionality is the bedrock of becoming courageous, so we must practice this as mothers with our children, as wives in our marriages, and as confidantes in our friendships.

The rhythm of the Courageous Girls discussion format fosters open relationships between moms and daughters, creating safe spaces where girls feel heard, known, and accepted. One of the moms in my group waited patiently for four years before her daughter began to share deeply with her. For years she built a foundation of trust but wondered why her daughter did not share much, especially at an emotional level. She just seemed uninterested or guarded. Then one day, after a hard day at school, they had the most touching moment. In that week the mother realized God had been preparing her to listen when her daughter needed her the most. We celebrated together because this signaled a turning point in their relationship.

We may not see the fruit of these investments in our daughters in everyday patterns of life. However, creating an open posture toward our children, where intimacy and vulnerability are embraced and encouraged, will pay off in the end. More importantly, it will give them tangible experiences of what these traits look like in relationship with God and others. How awesome it is when healthy relationships are practiced at home before it becomes necessary to model them as adults! Normalizing these processes early will help our daughters move through the teen and college years well.

At times it may seem impossible for moms to know how to comfort their daughters unless they received this training in their own childhood homes or experienced healthy relationships in adulthood. Learning how to comfort begins with tuning in to our own emotions. In fact, much of the trauma recovery process in professional counseling settings aims first to help people feel and then teaches them how to receive comfort from others. When we experience abuse or neglect, we are conditioned to believe that what we think, feel, need, or want *does not* and *should not* matter. It can take a woman many years to recover from the devastation of violation, so having grace for ourselves in the healing process is critical. In pursuing a deeply intentional relational journey with your daughter, you are already moving boldly and courageously toward healing and wholeness for yourself as well.

Growing up, I could rationalize any emotion I felt to the extent that it temporarily disappeared. Some of that is related to how I am wired. I successfully pushed past any feelings that tried to move into my reality. My skills in reframing difficulties served me well at times. I cautiously refer to this as the "athlete mentality"—no pain, no gain. There are some significant benefits to the athlete mentality that look like resilience and determination. Playing sports often teaches children how to commit to something they start, which positively affects future relationships and endeavors. Sports also help us learn the difference between discomfort and true injury, an important life skill. The danger presents itself when we ignore true injuries and live in denial, choosing to bury pain rather than regularly offering it back to God (and in many cases getting professional help). Throughout my education I played sports with injuries, all the while ignoring the pain in my body. I fell in love with volleyball and spent many years competing with a knee injury until I had no choice but to have my entire ACL repaired—ending my Olympic volleyball career track. (Okay, maybe just my high school career, but do not minimize the loss!)

There is a clear correlation between ignoring physical pain in the body and ignoring emotional or psychological pain.[7] Knowing how to identify and process our emotions and knowing how to connect with our bodies are intertwined; they are also connected to fully embracing our need for God. If we were made to tough it out on our own, why would we ever rely on help from our Creator or community? This is why emotional distress can make a person physically ill or cause long-term harm to the body. In the words of Shauna Niequist, author and speaker, "Many Christians, women especially, were raised to be obedient and easy, to swallow feelings, to choke down tears. This has not served us well. This has made it far too easy to injure our bodies and our souls in the name of good causes."[8] Amen, sister.

When I was younger, I learned to manage my anger, fear, and disappointment by escaping through eating, bingeing, purging, and compulsively exercising. I stumbled into this maladaptive coping strategy as a way to illegitimately comfort uncomfortable feelings. I used to say that Ben and Jerry were some of my best friends, especially in the form of Chunky Monkey. I have always had friends; I just didn't let them see me struggle. I had a deep unmet need to be heard and had not learned how to really talk with my friends, cry, or acknowledge anger. Instead, my body would feel anxiety and I would automatically reach for food or go for a really long run. It was overwhelming and, at times, all-consuming. I see the same pattern in many girls and women, regardless of natural wiring and personality, who have not been taught how to honor their emotions. Controlling food and being consumed by food, such as by rigid rule keeping or living for the next meal, are more subtle behaviors that provide a momentary quick fix through a hormone called dopamine. These behaviors and those of a similar nature create bondage and are often followed by crippling shame.[9]

Thankfully, in high school I learned to cope with my emotions through journaling. Journaling has been found to be helpful for all kinds of recovery work. In some ways it gave me at least one healthy outlet, albeit a secretive one, for all the emotions I felt throughout my teen years. As an adult who has spent years healing with God, I can look back over scribbled notes documenting my emotions and see the disconnect between my inner and outer worlds. I have learned so much about who I am and my basic human needs through this practice, and I know I am not alone. The cry to be heard and find comfort is repeated in my office by every girl, teen, and woman who has ever been in touch with her heart. The amazing news is that comfort can be provided in many forms. However, one of the most satisfying and relief-producing ways to receive comfort is through the arms of a loving mother who accepts her daughter as she is and provides steadfast strength that reminds her all will be okay.

SHE RUNS TOWARD EMOTIONS, NOT AWAY

Courageous Girls—moms and daughters—practice engaging their emotions regularly. They learn how to handle their emotions and those of others with care. They regard one another with tenderness and utilize healthy coping strategies. If we learn how to process and regulate our emotions in appropriate ways, especially in the safety of our homes as we grow up, we will meet our God-given emotional needs in legitimate ways. If we do not learn this skill, we will leak emotional waste and try to meet our needs in illegitimate ways. At the core, most maladaptive behaviors are a desperate cry for empathy and compassion. This is why the key component of Courageous Girls is community. We need one another on every level. We need to learn to identify our needs at every point on the emotional continuum, and we do this by listening to and learning from the experiences of others.

In a special way, Courageous Girls are mirrors for one another. Over time and with healthy adult models who are willing to walk through these practices repeatedly, each girl can learn to regulate her emotions in productive and safe ways. All children need this support; truthfully, many adults do too. Regulating emotions is so difficult, especially when we have not been taught to recognize or voice them.

Emotions are like trains; they move quickly. That is why they are called *emotions*—you can bank on the fact that there will be movement and constant flux. Some days they will be in check; other days they will veer off track. They may even run you over on occasion! We need to remember that emotions do not control us, but they help guide us to a more authentic self and connection with God and others. We need to grasp the depths of our sorrows in order to feel the height of our joys.

Unlike emotions, the love of God is constant. It is unmovable and never-changing, regardless of how we feel in the moment. We need to know how to ask for help, especially from a loving God; accepting our need for a Savior is the foundation of our faith. When we have trouble regulating our emotions, we can turn to God and remember this: "The LORD your God is with you, the Mighty Warrior who saves. He will take great delight in you; in his love he will no longer rebuke you, but will rejoice over you with singing" (Zeph. 3:17).

Takeaway

Journaling is one way to learn or relearn how to identify, express, and share your emotions. Open a blank notebook and begin on the first page. For many of us, knowing what to write about is the toughest part. Try this: Sit quietly with God for ten minutes. Don't do, say, or read anything. Just pay attention. Notice your thoughts. What thoughts or scenes are moving through your mind? Notice your body. What part of your body is tense? Notice your environment. What do you see, smell, hear, taste, feel? Then read Psalm 139:23-24, and ask God to search you and help you see whether there are any anxieties of which you are unaware. Write down impressions that come to mind. Then recognize that you are not alone in what you are carrying, and ask God to lead you toward comfort.

Take It a Step Further

Start a mother/daughter journal too. Share things with each other when you need or want to. After writing a message, leave the journal on your daughter's bed for her to read it in her own time. Let her know that she can do the same, leaving her thoughts for you on your bed. Allow this tool to be a way to communicate on a deeper level, especially if tough conversations are new or haven't gone well in the past. There is safety in writing down our feelings before we give voice to them. Practice doing this together and watch your relationship flourish.

4

She Tunes In to the Voice of Grace

He sees you. He knows you.
Ellie Holcomb, Christa Wells, and Nicole Witt, "You Are Loved"

That you may love the LORD your God, listen
to his voice, and hold fast to him.
Deuteronomy 30:20

C. S. Lewis once wrote, "I believe in Christianity as I believe that the Sun has risen, not only because I see it, but because by it I see everything else."[1] What lens do you look through? Many women think their value is found in their appearance, performance, or good choices. The voices that say "I will never be good enough, smart enough, or pretty enough" haunt them. Some feel as if they have to hide their true selves because if others really knew them, they would be rejected. If we are honest, to some extent we all try to be what our husbands want, parents dreamed of, or churches communicate we should be. When we do this, anxiety rages. Our hearts are pulled in every direction, and we are left wanting to shut down or run away from others' expectations and needs. It is just a matter of time before we burn out.

We can all relate to burnout at some point in our stories. Maybe you are the stay-at-home mom who dreamed of doing something mighty for Jesus' kingdom but feels worn and used up. Maybe you are now retired and look back on your life with nothing but despair, exhaustion, and cynicism. Or maybe you are the single thirty-year-old who finds herself feeling as if she's an outsider to the family club at church. You might even be the pastor's wife or ministry leader who can help everyone else out of a crisis but has no one to help you. Each of these situations reveals not only burnout but also the realities of women who have focused on the expectations of others rather than on God's purpose for their lives. Expectations whisper from every part of society, and unless we silence them in our lives, they will not be quiet. Teaching our daughters how to discern the voice of the one true God starts with modeling how to evaluate whose voice is truly worthy.

SHE KNOWS HER VALUE

One day my oldest child asked me why I chose to be a counselor and inquired whether I enjoy going to work. At the time all I could say was that I am so honored to be a part of God's miracles through the transformation of people's lives. In my practice I have heard woman after woman share her experience with her mom who either was ill-equipped to coach her daughter to listen to God's voice or perpetuated lies to her daughter with loud and cruel words. One woman shared that it has taken her forty years to replace her mom's voice with the voice of God, simply because her "Christian" mom confused and abused her so deeply. I hear stories of dads who could not be brave enough to risk inadequacy to pursue their daughters' hearts and lacked tenderness, presence, and leadership. As a professional counselor, I have the opportunity to be a part of mending broken hearts and watching people experience God's life-changing love. In the end, my career has taught me how to love my girls well. I responded to my daughter's question, "Yes, I love going to work, but even more, I love being your mom." I want to live unencumbered by the voices of others and model that freedom in Christ to my children. Jesus' voice is the only one that is able to give us what we desperately need.

One of my favorite biblical narratives tells an account of a misunderstood individual known as the Samaritan woman. Since she had been married five times, I assume her situation provided rich content for local gossip. Even today there are various commentaries around her situation: Did she have so many husbands because she was adulterous or widowed? Regardless, I can imagine the burdens she carried. Surely surrounded by the unhelpful voices of others, she kept her head down in shame.

The Samaritan woman frequented a well outside the city to fetch water. Given the hostilities between Jews and Samaritans at that time, we can be certain that this was a well visited only by the Samaritan people. But one day Jesus, a Jewish traveler, boldly made His way to the well. In doing so, He defied many cultural norms of His day. Samaritan women were viewed as lowly as rabid dogs by some members of the community, but Jesus did not care. Even though she was a woman and a Samaritan, He looked her in the eye and conversed with her. I wonder whether the Samaritan woman could look Jesus in the eye as she grappled with all the voices of guilt, shame, and dishonor she had heard over the years.

During His conversation with her, Jesus asked the Samaritan woman for a drink of water. Cryptically, He told her that if she knew the gift of God and who asked her for a drink at the well, she would have asked Him for living water that would cause her to thirst no more. Naturally, the woman was intrigued. The ensuing conversation reveals that Jesus knew the woman was cohabiting with a man to whom she was not married, a disgraceful move for her time. But Jesus saw past her actions and into her heart. Seeing that she was searching for more but with no hope of finding it, He told her that He could give her what she needed. His voice, the truth, led her to fulfillment. The story ends with the woman returning to her village to tell the whole town about her afternoon with Jesus. The Bible tells us that many more came to believe Jesus was the Messiah because of her boldness and courage (see John 4:4–42).

Like the Samaritan woman, we are all trying to quench our deepest thirsts by listening to the voices of others. We live in a world where the prince of lies roars like a lion to find his prey (see 1 Pet. 5:8). He uses all the cultural norms, the tragedies in our lives, and the narratives in our heads to try to drown out the voice of love. It does not take much to get us off track from the truth of God's grace and hope for our lives. The lies and shame messages can consume us. Courageous Girls helps mothers and daughters discern the difference between what God says and what the world and its prince subtly communicate. A Courageous Girl can discern God's voice.

SHE KNOWS HER SHEPHERD'S VOICE

Often it can seem as if hearing God's voice is reserved for spiritual giants. For some it may feel too mystical or charismatic. But having a personal relationship with God means communicating with Him. I cannot imagine feeling close to my husband if we never spoke or if I did all the talking. (That may happen on occasion but not on a regular basis.) According to God's Word and the experience of many of His children, we have a direct line to Him. You may be wondering whether He speaks only in an audible voice. Not necessarily. God speaks through the Bible, our community, creation, our intuitions, and more. I think that the way we hear God is directly linked to our wiring. Learning our unique communication style with God is part of the maturing experience within intimacy. Hearing does not always mean we understand what God is saying, but recognizing and being attuned to His voice are the starting points. Let's use the analogy of a baby in a mama's womb to better understand the power of tuning in to God's voice amid all the world's noise. Parenting.com shared this information:

> Doctors assumed that babies were born without any knowledge about the outside world. But recent research is questioning this assumption, offering clues to what babies comprehend in utero, what they remember after they're born, and how that information prepares them for the world outside the womb.…
>
> The uterus isn't exactly the quietest place to hang out. Not only can a baby hear the sounds of his mom's body—her stomach growling, her heart beating, the occasional hiccup or burp—but he can also hear noises from beyond.…
>
> Of course, not all sounds are the same. Perhaps the most significant one a baby hears in utero is his mother's voice. Around the seventh and eighth month, a fetus's heart rate slows down slightly whenever his mother is speaking, indicating that mom's voice has a calming effect.[2]

What would it be like to be so close and intimate with our Creator that, like babies in the womb, what we hear in His presence prepares us for the outside world? Not only might we learn to pause when we hear Him speaking, allowing the calming effect of His truth to pierce our anxious ways, but we also might be able to discern His voice above all the other noises around us. And there is a lot of noise!

Tuning out the voices in our heads and in the world around us is one of the most profound disciplines in the Christian walk. It changes everything, especially our perspective. Thanks to my systems training as a marriage and family therapist and the reframing skills my parents instilled in me, I have a natural inclination to pause and consider the context of any thought, experience, or message. Our basic beliefs about God, ourselves, and the purpose of this life shape all our decisions today. Our views are birthed out of our cultural experiences, combined with our unique wiring, and we all must hold them up to what God says. The woman who practices using the Word of God as her lens has a firm foundation. There is no stopping that Courageous Girl!

John 10:1–16 in *The Message* says,

> Let me set this before you as plainly as I can. If a person climbs over or through the fence of a sheep pen instead of going through the gate, you know he's up to no good—a sheep rustler! The shepherd walks right up to the gate. The gatekeeper opens the gate to him and the sheep recognize his voice. He calls his own sheep by name and leads them out. When he gets them all out, he leads them and they follow because they are familiar with his voice. They won't follow a stranger's voice but will scatter because they aren't used to the sound of it....

I'll be explicit, then. I am the Gate for the sheep. All those others are up to no good—sheep stealers, every one of them. But the sheep didn't listen to them. I am the Gate. Anyone who goes through me will be cared for—will freely go in and out, and find pasture. A thief is only there to steal and kill and destroy. I came so they can have real and eternal life, more and better life than they ever dreamed of.

I am the Good Shepherd. The Good Shepherd puts the sheep before himself, sacrifices himself if necessary. A hired man is not a real shepherd. The sheep mean nothing to him. He sees a wolf come and runs for it, leaving the sheep to be ravaged and scattered by the wolf. He's only in it for the money. The sheep don't matter to him.

I am the Good Shepherd. I know my own sheep and my own sheep know me. In the same way, the Father knows me and I know the Father. I put the sheep before myself, sacrificing myself if necessary. You need to know that I have other sheep in addition to those in this pen. I need to gather and bring them, too. They'll also recognize my voice. Then it will be one flock, one Shepherd.

There is so much profundity in this passage, in which Jesus called Himself the Good Shepherd. In Jesus' day, shepherds' primary responsibility was to care for and protect their sheep. They were so intimately aware of each individual sheep, to the point of being able to distinguish differences between the many in their flocks. What's more amazing, sheep could discern their shepherd's call even if they were mingling with other herds. This is a powerful analogy, as Jesus distinguished Himself from the Pharisees and declared that He is the gate. Through this analogy Jesus claimed He is the *only* way to eternal and abundant life. Unlike the enemy, who comes to steal, kill, and destroy (see v. 10), Jesus came to give life abundant. The only power the enemy really has is to distract Jesus' followers from His voice by sending wolves into the sheep's pen.

The voices we hear in our heads are beliefs or schemas we develop from our life experiences and the influences around us. For example, if I trip over a curb, the voice in my head might tell me, *You are so clumsy,* or I might just laugh at myself and move on. The narrative is based on whose opinion I rely on. We all develop these thinking patterns, even though we are not fully conscious of them and don't know how they develop. Sometimes the voices in our heads are simple misinterpretations, but sometimes they are restatements from influential people. In moments of difficulty, those we trust the most can have greater influence on how we interpret life experiences. When those relationships are positive, they can help align us with grace. But when they're negative, the effects can be devastating. For example, a coach who tells your daughter, "You will never be good enough" and fails to reinforce her other strengths can have negative long-term effects on her psyche. Having the kind of mother who walks alongside her and helps her discern God's voice is enormously vital to her long-term healing. This is when we have to help our daughters evaluate whose voice is the loudest: the coach's or God's?

One of our main jobs as parents is to help our daughters discern the voice of God and create space for them to hear His voice repeatedly so that, like a baby in the womb, they can recognize it quickly. Quiet time—though an overutilized, Christian-centric phrase—is still a crucial spiritual discipline. When we recognize why we need to tune in to the Word of God, the muscle that helps us discern God's voice from the world's grows stronger. Modeling this rhythm and practicing it with our daughters help them build sustainable habits and live out of the greatness of God's love for them.

I once heard the analogy of being like a pickle. A pickle is a cucumber that has been marinated in brine for at least twenty-four hours. Dipping a cucumber in brine once a week will not create a pickle. Similarly, being in the Word once a week will hardly transform us. Creating healthy habits that are woven into the DNA of our Courageous Girls requires the recognition that it takes ten thousand hours to become an expert in something. According to leadership expert Malcolm Gladwell, it's the magic number for those who achieve greatness in their fields.[3] What could happen if we applied this statistic to our time in the Word? We have to submerge ourselves wholly until we see the world through a biblical lens. Marinate, ladies. There is nothing like a juicy dill pickle!

The authors of *The Cure* remind us that what we believe about ourselves is a direct correlation of what we believe about our God.[4] Former theology professor at Seattle Pacific University, Dr. Kerry Dearborn, added, "And what we believe about our God tells us more about what we believe about ourselves."[5] Both are true. Our views of God and ourselves inform the way we live and the choices we make. Our beliefs influence how we act and therefore inform how we feel. Remember how I said in chapter 3 that if we overemphasize our thoughts, we can dishonor our emotions? Once we acknowledge that emotions are a part of experiencing the fullness of God and are not meant to be dismissed, we can reunite our belief systems with the skill of leading our behaviors and our emotions. When these three are aligned, we develop integrity, which shrinks the gap between whom we profess ourselves to be and how we live. This takes great intentionality and awareness. Romans 12:1–2 says, "I urge you, brothers and sisters, in view of God's mercy, to offer your bodies as a living sacrifice, holy and pleasing to God—this is your true and proper worship. Do not conform to the pattern of this world, but be transformed by the renewing of your mind. Then you will be able to test and approve what God's will is—his good, pleasing and perfect will." I urge you, sister, in view of God's mercy, let's give all of who we are to God—our emotions, our bodies, *and* our minds. We are a confused flock in need of a Shepherd.

Have you ever heard yourself or another say, "My heart is telling me one thing, but my mind is saying another"? We can feel pulled in different directions even within ourselves. God's Word is the leader, and our minds are the ones who send the marching orders to the rest of our beings. We can help our bodies and emotions catch up to where our minds meditate on God's truth. The Bible says, "We demolish arguments and every pretension that sets itself up against the knowledge of God, and we take captive every thought to make it obedient to Christ" (2 Cor. 10:5). Neuroscientific research only validates what the Scriptures have been instructing us to do all along. In the *Huffington Post*, Ashley Turner wrote, "Meditation is perhaps the most crucial instrument to harness the power of thought, culti-vate more peace, clarity and happiness. Learning to train the brain and focus our attention is crucial to thriving and cultivating a peak performance in any endeavor. Long-time psychotherapist Dr. Ron Alexander ... speaks of MIND STRENGTH, or the resiliency, effi-cacy and emotional intelligence that arise as we begin the process of controlling the mind. Mind strength is one of the most empowering tools we can employ to impact and improve all aspects of life."[6] This is not a new concept, though the research behind it is recent.

For thousands of years, Christians have been meditating. Meditation simply means to contemplate or reflect on something. The key difference between Christian meditation and other forms of spiritual meditation is that the first has us fill our minds with Christ and the latter has us empty our minds. Philippians 4:8 says, "Finally,

[Courageous Mama], whatever is true, whatever is honorable, whatever is right, whatever is pure, whatever is lovely, whatever is of good repute, if there is any excellence and if anything worthy of praise, dwell on these things" (NASB). The apostle Paul went on to say in verse 9, "Whatever you have learned or received or heard from me, or seen in me—put it into practice. And the God of peace will be with you." Can we imagine being so completely soaked in God's presence that we could tell our daughters to copy us? This is a sobering thought.

To summarize, science is proving that the power of meditation means taking space between thoughts and actions.[7] For centuries Christians have been reading God's Word, memorizing Scripture, and meditating on its wisdom to navigate life. The core of our purpose in parenting is to tell our children who God is and who they are according to His Word. This is why we read our Bibles—to curl up in the arms of our Father like a newborn baby and listen to His voice apart from all the others.

You know the voices that compete with God's. Facebook. Instagram. Netflix. Superstars. Church. Christian stars. Girlfriends. Spouses. Family. Teachers. Bullies. Bosses. The list goes on. Being attuned to God's voice takes time and diligence, and it's a primary goal of raising a daughter rooted in grace. God's voice is not critical, judgmental, harsh, or controlling. It's also not wholly permissive, dissociated, or ambivalent. Instead, it's a voice full of love: "Never Stopping, Never Giving Up, Unbreaking, Always and Forever Love."[8] A Courageous Girl is able to hear this voice of love and through it discern what is true about God, herself, and those around her.

SHE LETS GOD LIFT HER HEAD UP

For years, when I looked in the mirror, I thought I was ugly. Though I moved past the behaviors of bulimia once I confessed to my parents, the thought patterns about my appearance still haunted me. My journey toward healing has helped me empathize with so many over the years. Looking back, I remember the struggle of waking up in the morning; my first thought—*I am ugly*—informed how I prepared for the day. I would fixate on what I should wear, how to style my hair, or how to apply my makeup. I was completely consumed by my outer appearance. Some days I would throw my hands in the air and give up, then put on a hat, sweats, and a baggy sweatshirt instead. In either case, I was unable to enjoy the gifts throughout my day as I meditated on my appearance.

In college I decided to take the challenge of a professor. I posted a sticky note on my dorm mirror that said, "I am fearfully and wonderfully made" (Ps. 139:14). For ninety days straight, I read that verse out loud and purposed to take my thoughts captive. In that ninety-day period, God began to change my beliefs. I recall the morning when I stood before the mirror and the thought *I am beautiful* popped into my head. It was not a vain, conceited thought, but it was as if I heard and agreed with the Father as He delighted in my appearance. That moment changed the rest of my actions that day and in the weeks following. I took less time to get ready in the mornings while still valuing my body by showering and making myself presentable. The time it took to get ready decreased, and my focus on others increased. I was no longer engulfed in my thoughts, and I began to truly embrace His voice in Psalm 139. The odd thing is that no one ever told me I was ugly. In fact, quite the opposite. There was no human that could quench the desire of my heart to be beautiful. Instead, I needed to experience the Father gently lifting my head, speaking His truth over me.

Danger lurks in the places where we make our identity into something other than what God intended. If we do not know the Word well, we can go to others who have walked with God a little longer and can help us discern His ways. A Bible study can help us grow. Meeting with other Courageous Mamas or mentors can help too. Doing a devotional with our daughters is beneficial to both mom and daughter. And, of course, prayer can be a powerful way to discern God's voice. Get into the habit of asking Him to show you whether something is of Him or of the world. He is faithful to answer.

SHE RECOGNIZES GRACE OVER PERFORMANCE

The essence of our faith is that we are loved. You are loved. Your daughter is loved. I have spent many years trying to earn love by being the best daughter, wife, leader, mom, friend, speaker, and counselor. I am done with that way of being, and I invite you to be done as well. I have officially declared that I no longer need to earn anyone's love, because God says so. He took care of everything we would ever need on the cross. If I try to earn His grace by measuring up to someone else's expectation, I exhaust valuable energy that I could be using to show grace to others. Getting us to try to prove ourselves worthy of love is a clever tactic the enemy uses to keep us ineffective. As we wake up to a new day every morning, God proves that He is for us. His grace is undeserved favor. Our job is to plug ourselves into relationship and let Him do the rest!

The essence of the Christian faith is that "by grace you have been saved" (Eph. 2:5). This truth never ceases to amaze me as I pause and remember the kindness of God. It is because of grace, not my own efforts, that I have been chosen, pursued, and redeemed. Before I understood the power of grace, I was tormented by the compulsion to please others. I was caught in the trap of performance-based Christianity—much like the sticker trap in Max Lucado's book. I tried so hard to be all I could be—but for the sake of what? I still do not know, but I see the same struggles permeating the women around me. Once in a while, I find a Lucia who stands out, and I can discern the grace surrounding her. She has tasted and seen that the Lord is good and can be trusted (see Ps. 34:8).

The word *grace* (*chen* in Hebrew, *charis* in Greek) means "favor."[9] In our case, it means "undeserved favor." God stoops down toward us because He is love and kindness; He makes a way for us to be loved, known, and accepted. Though I began my relationship with Christ as a young girl, I did not understand "saved by grace" until my twenties. Somehow, between my upbringing, my wiring, and the Christian teachings in my circles, I learned to be a good Christian by *striving* to be like Jesus instead of allowing God to conform me to His image. If you have been in the church for a while, you might struggle with that statement. However, the enemy is like a wolf in sheep's clothing. He takes a truth in God's Word and, with a little manipulation, twists it into something God never intended. This is similar to steering a ship, as the slightest change in coordinates will create a major shift in the ship's course and, ultimately, its destination.

As mamas raising daughters we dearly love, we might give in to the voice that says we should raise respectful, obedient, polite girls who know their Bible and make good choices. Or, on the other side, you might be drawn to the messages "Be you" and "Who cares what anyone else thinks? You are enough." Even the Disney message "Trust your heart" sounds good. We must think critically, asking, "Is this what Jesus really meant when He saved us by grace alone? And how do we teach truth to our daughters so that they will not be caught in the same traps?" Remember these truths: Jesus is enough; I am broken; I cannot earn grace, but He makes me enough. That is what Jesus does.

We teach grace to our daughters like a slow drip coming from a runny faucet; we talk about it, offer undeserved favor, and model it. We talk about offering grace to siblings, friends, and others in the community. We discuss that no one is perfect and practice praying for help when our daughters feel overwhelmed or insufficient. We teach them to turn to God and watch for the ways He shows up. We pray for God to fill in the cracks because He is enough.

In the throes of parenthood and life, it's easy to wake up each day with our sense of worth based on what we accomplished and the state of our children. We may measure their behaviors and development by how they are perceived by their teachers, Sunday school leaders, other parents, and, of course, our in-laws. Since the advent of social media and reality TV, like *American Idol* and *So You Think You Can Dance*, the next generation has become even more focused on becoming famous and followed in a way no one could have imagined fifteen years ago. It's remarkable how cultural norms have created a deep impulse to perform and wait for the likes.

If Jesus lived in the twenty-first century, I doubt He would be on social media. That is not a judgment statement about whether or not we should be using social media but rather an informed conclusion based on whom I have come to know Jesus to be and on His heart for us. He is countercultural yet so relevant to our basic needs. He often said "Do not tell anyone I am doing this" because He trusted the timing of others' discovery. We seem incapable of moving through our day until we tell everyone in our social media circles what we are doing. The younger we are, the more vulnerable we are to the web of messages in our societies. This may cause us to pause and seriously consider at what age our daughters should be allowed to use social media. This will be different for each family and for each daughter, but when we do let them, they need our regular coaching to help them discern how to use the platforms in healthy ways.

Coaching means we provide general guideposts to help our daughters navigate new and potentially damaging roads. The authors of *The Cure & Parents* said it this way: "A guideline is worthless to a one-year-old, but wonderfully life-giving to a ten-year-old. It gives more direction than directives. It employs a principle, a way of seeing, to help children understand how to navigate a variety of life decisions. The guideline is relationally communicated, allowing children to own their choices in heartfelt obedience rather than compliance to a rule. It communicates consequences and the basis, protection, and freedom within the truth being given."[10] This is why the Courageous Girls curriculum is so powerful—because a mom can have regular conversations throughout her daughter's young life that will strengthen her ability to navigate new choices ahead of her. Rules, or rigid theology, tell her what to do but never equip her for a time when the rules are not clear. We need to raise daughters who are able to think through their own choices before they act and can live with the consequences of what they choose. This intentional way of being helps Courageous Girls own their decisions, discern potential danger, and lean in to their relationship with God long after they are grown.

SHE KNOWS THE DIFFERENCE BETWEEN GRACE AND SHAME MESSAGES

Many of the issues we and our daughters struggle with are rooted in shame. We seek approval from others because God designed us with a longing to be seen, known, and accepted. We have the privilege of helping our daughters understand that only Jesus can quench this thirst. To learn this lesson, some girls will need to explore other waters so that they can compare the difference between true and false fulfillment. In any case, they get to choose whether they will receive grace or accept shame.

In her book *Daring Greatly*, Brené Brown said, "[Shame] is … the fear that something we've done or failed to do, an ideal that we've not lived up to, or a goal that we've not accomplished makes us unworthy of connection.... *Shame is the intensely painful feeling or experience of believing that we are flawed and therefore unworthy of love and belonging.*"[11] When we mess up or see our limitations in life, we can be in tune enough to experience conviction that compels us to change our behavior. We are loved and still mess up sometimes. One passage in Scripture that is most dear to me gives voice to Paul, a former Pharisee who had to keep all the laws, who recounted how God used his limitations and weaknesses to keep him connected to grace. He wrote,

> Because of the extravagance of those revelations, and so I wouldn't get a big head, I was given the gift of a handicap to keep me in constant touch with my limitations. Satan's angel did his best to get me down; what he in fact did was push me to my knees. No danger then of walking around high and mighty! At first I didn't think of it as a gift, and begged God to remove it. Three times I did that, and then he told me,
>
> > My grace is enough; it's all you need.
> > My strength comes into its own in your weakness.
>
> Once I heard that, I was glad to let it happen. I quit focusing on the handicap and began appreciating the gift. It was a case of Christ's strength moving in on my weakness. Now I take limitations in stride, and with good cheer, these limitations that cut me down to size—abuse, accidents, opposition, bad breaks. I just let Christ take over! And so the weaker I get, the stronger I become. (2 Cor. 12:7–10 THE MESSAGE)

First, let me acknowledge that many have misunderstood Paul's words in this passage. I want to clarify that Paul's thorn was *not* an abusive relationship. Paul was talking about something in his humanity that limited him from fully giving what he wanted to give to God. We do not know what this thorn was, though many have guessed, but weakness was not the point. Instead of wallowing in shame, Paul called his limitation a "gift of a handicap." Staying in tune with our vulnerabilities and knowing we are loved are right in the pocket of grace.

The enemy wanted Paul to blame God. Paul could have said, "God hates me. I am not good enough. God is punishing me. I deserve better than this. I am unlovable." Instead, Paul knew God's heart and was attuned to His voice. He heard the Father speak over him, "My grace is enough; it's all you need. My strength comes into its own in your weakness" (v. 9). The NIV says, "My grace is sufficient for you, for my power is made perfect in weakness." We have no need to hide our struggles, limitations, or handicaps. As courageous mothers and daughters, we can be confident that His power fills in the cracks of our brokenness.

SHE SEES THE RAINBOWS OF HIS PROMISE

When I was in college in the late 1990s, I was on a run to Gas Works Park in Seattle, Washington. Like most days, it was cloudy. On this particular day, the clouds seemed heavier and drearier, reflecting the weight of my soul. Even though it was probably misting, the raindrops felt like pellets on my face. I felt so alone and deeply troubled by the addictive behaviors of my eating disorder. I cried the whole way to the park and then stood on a mound overlooking the water. My heart lamented, *I don't want this anymore!* As I looked up, the sky parted and the sun peeked its face through the clouds. Blue sky shone through directly over my mound. I felt the warmth on my cheeks as I wiped my tears. I looked around; it was raining everywhere I looked except right where I was standing. A rainbow soon appeared, and I was reminded of God's promise to Noah (see Gen. 9:12–16). God spoke to me through the rainbow.

Though the sun quickly disappeared and I jogged back to my dorm room in the pouring rain, my perspective had completely changed. God heard my cry and touched my soul. To this day, I can feel it in my body when I recall this memory. Through that experience, He showed me that the rain showers of our lives serve a purpose. While He will not always remove them, He will be present throughout them, giving us moments of warmth that sustain us through the storm. That day in Gas Works Park, I learned I was not alone. God showed me He is with me, painting a tangible truth in my spirit—the arc of my very own rainbow.

My daughters and I talk about rainbows regularly. We often remark how curious it is that rainbows require both rain and sunshine for such a beautiful phenomenon to occur. Such is life. The moments of amazing wonder, the grace that sustains us in hardship, the fact we are never alone—all these realities can help us keep our footing when the storm comes. A Courageous Girl can discern God's voice and live according to the grace and hope of His ways.

Takeaway

List all the lies you are tempted to believe about yourself, about others, and about God. Sometimes we do not even know they are lies because we have accepted them as truth. Once you write a list, identify where each one may have originated in your story. Ask God to show you whether these voices are aligned with His truths, and if they are not, search for Scripture passages to counter the voice that you are tempted to believe. Commit to memorizing one of the Scriptures you find with your daughter, and meditate on its truth for ninety days. See what God's power does in and through your weakness.

Take It a Step Further

Write out a time line of your story. List all the events in your life, good and bad, and identify what age you were during each event. Consider sharing your time line with another person. See whether you can discover any other shame-based beliefs life has taught you. Then bring all these events and beliefs to the foot of the cross.

5

She Knows Who She Is in Community

The person who loves their dream of community will destroy community, but the person who loves those around them will create community.
Dietrich Bonhoeffer, *Life Together*

We have all felt alone at some point in our lives, sometimes in the midst of a crowd of people we call friends. Traveling the road of motherhood, especially in the earlier years, can be some of the longest, loneliest times. Throughout many years of private practice, I have listened to women share how hard it is to find friends they really trust. The void of authentic friendships in their lives leaves them uncertain and insecure about how to coach their daughters to foster relationships and manage other natural dilemmas that arise in female friendships. How do we handle mean girls? How do we prevent the formation of cliques? How do we find a best friend who will be faithful? What does a healthy friendship even look like?

No matter our place in life, we all have a need to be seen and valued and to belong; it's knit into the fabric of who we are. The desire to have a small tribe we call our own is common to all women. *No matter how introverted or independent we claim to be, we all long for a landing place where we can be ourselves.* Jesus invites us as Christians into the deep waters of faith, and this often looks like intentional community.

SHE JOURNEYS IN COMMUNITY

Within those deep waters of faith is the space where relationships between women are created and nurtured. We all long for it, yet many of us only dip our toes in the shallow end. Women have a difficult time, to say the least, standing firm and being confident in female relationships. We approach relationships cautiously, hiding behind our masks and politely extending stiff arms to one another. The undercurrent of competitiveness and comparison cultivates insecurity, provoking women to bolt rather than move toward one another. Our caution with female relationships can be exhausting, and just giving up is a tempting alternative. Ironically, clinical research shows that women generally desire closer emotional relationships than men. We have a great capacity to be known and to know one another, yet at the depths of our souls, we fear this vulnerability. This fear causes us to sabotage relationships, sometimes even before they begin, with gossip, surface interactions, busyness, pleasing, avoidance, and more. If God created women with a deep desire for relational connection, why do we resist?

I have heard many women confess that they do not invest in female relationships to avoid drama. I assure you, if you are raising a daughter, you will be required to interact with other girls and their moms who regularly find themselves in the middle of this kind of relating. Drama does not have to be the end-all. In fact, it can be a catalyst for change (good or bad) in each of us. *Drama* can be defined as "an exciting, emotional, or unexpected event or circumstance."[1] Most people love a good drama series on Netflix because it's packed with interesting characters and plot twists. Perhaps we can view living in community with others in a similar way.

When I read the Gospels, I find a lot of drama. Personally I could do without it, but when I remember that Jesus said all the laws depend on our love for God and others (see Matt. 22:37–40), I cannot deny that community is part of His plan. I want to help the next generation of girls, who are growing up in some of the most emotionally disconnected days in history, live as Jesus intended. This means they must be rooted in community. That begins with us finding or creating community wherever we go. Our girls will have an easier time embracing healthy community if we decide to go there first.

Whether we always seem to find ourselves in the middle of betrayal and hurtful relationships or whether we've developed some clever coping strategies to protect ourselves from being hurt by others, we must face our fears and dive into the deep waters of community together. This is part of the reason why Courageous Girls groups ask moms to be involved *and* committed to one another over a long period of time. Courageous Girls groups are not like other groups; we are deeply intentional, long-term communities of mothers and daughters who fearlessly address every issue that shapes the lives of girls today. Through years of practice, we aim to build healthy community before our daughters leave home. This group is one where moms and daughters go deep in relationship with each other, with female peers, and with God. Even dads will learn to have more meaningful relationships with their wives and other dads as they intentionally pursue their girls.

Humans are designed for intimacy—to be known and to know another. Trust is an essential ingredient of intimacy but can be built only with time, consistency, and, ironically, conflict. Most relationships do not arrive at conflict until two years into knowing each other.[2] This is around the point when the honeymoon stage ends. Many of us jump ship long before we get to see what God will do post-honeymoon and post-conflict. The journey of mothering girls is a journey of humility, one where we get the privilege (yes, privilege) of seeing ourselves in a new light as we participate in shrinking the gap between whom we say we want to be and who we actually are, as well as between what we say we want for our daughters and what we actually teach them.

SHE GOES WHERE HER TRUST IS WITHOUT BORDERS

One of my all-time favorite worship songs is "Oceans." I love the whole song, but there are a couple of lines that God will not let me shake:

> Spirit, lead me where my trust is without borders....
> Take me deeper than my feet could ever wander.[3]

My prayer is that He takes us Courageous Mamas to places where our trust is without borders.

Being known in community is necessarily one of these places because it requires intense vulnerability. Authentically participating in community requires us to trust God and others without reservation. It requires humility and the release of our clever coping strategies to hide. Trust draws us in to meet our deepest needs to be known and loved as we are.[4] So what keeps us from leaving the shore?

Acting courageously in a sea of women can be like swimming among bloodthirsty sharks in treacherous waters; most of us know this because we have been hurt by other females. I cannot tell you how many moms ask how to help their little girls navigate this "mean girl syndrome." If you wrestle with this issue, you are not alone. Courageous Girls groups are a response to those cries. As a fellow mom in the trenches, counseling, living out community, and learning from moms who have gone before us, I am here to tell you that we can do this! Every generation has had some sort of battle before them. Eric Metaxas, historical and political author, said that though things look and feel really bad around us, the truth is that every generation since the time of Christ has thought it was the "end" of their time. However, God always raises up a remnant for His kingdom purposes.[5] The good news is that God is ever present and will raise up strong believers who stand firm in their faith to be a light in a dark world. Mamas, it is not by chance you are reading this book. We, alongside our daughters, can be those strong believers shining light to a dark world for such a time as this!

SHE'S NOT ALONE

Since the emergence of the digital age, while our community has broadened to global levels, our feelings of loneliness have increased. Technology is helpful for many reasons but has also contributed to the declining ability of girls (and boys) to meet their God-designed relational needs. The phenomenon worsens with each generation overly exposed to screen life. From the ways our brains develop to how we learn social cues, social platforms and digital devices create a negative return on societal investment. Their excessive use contributes to increased levels of bullying, depression, anxiety, insecurity, and addiction. Researchers believe the digital invasion has become one of the greatest attacks on relationships and authentic community.[6] Relationship data says humans are created for fewer and committed friendships, reaffirming there is a point when we truly max out on the number of people we can manage in our lives.[7] In light of this ever-changing paradigm, our daughters need tangible examples of what it means to love, trust, serve, and move through life with a few trusted individuals. Developing a Courageous Girls group is one way to practice this.

Choosing to join a group of moms and daughters for three to twelve years might sound intimidating, cultish, stifling, or exclusive. It's truly none of the above. Jesus modeled something profound with regard to community. He chose to invite twelve random men, who each had their own issues, to live in intentional community for three years. These men did not know Jesus was asking them to follow Him for three years exactly, but they knew Jesus was asking them for a commitment. These misfits were handpicked and individually invited to follow Jesus. When they received their invitations, they hardly knew Him. Even so, they said yes to His call. I believe they were longing for something more.

Jesus had only twelve disciples. He and those twelve ministered to thousands. Together they wept, prayed, served, laughed, ate, walked side by side, and listened to one another. Among the twelve, Jesus even had a few with whom He was more intimate. According to the disciple John, he was "the disciple whom Jesus loved" (John 21:20). That's a pretty funny thought, isn't it? Jesus was closer to some than others, which gives His followers permission to be vulnerable with a few while loving and serving the many around us. This may come at a high cost. One of those close friends, Judas Iscariot, betrayed Him. Anticipating this action, Jesus responded by washing His betrayer's feet while he was still among the inner circle of friends (see John 13:2–5). Jesus saw the war inside Judas and served him anyway; this is a reflection of the gift, complexity, and cost of community living.

Given the cost of community, the temptation to hide and remain alone in life is completely understandable. Many Christians are afraid to be seen as exclusive, and that is the right heart posture. However, a fear of exclusivity can also become a rather clever way to avoid the risk of being fully known and loved by others. This was me. One of my best friends confronted me in the earlier years of our friendship with a statement that was hard to hear. She said that I had a gift of making everyone feel as if they were my best friend, but it left my closest friends feeling insecure about their place in my life. It was cause for me to pause. Was making everyone my best friend what Jesus meant when He instructed us to love others as He loves us? (see John 13:34). Or was I just avoiding the chance of ever being betrayed by a Judas by cleverly staying safe in my friendliness?

Through prayer and intentional risk, I changed my approach to relationships. I asked female acquaintances to join me in my efforts to raise courageous girls. I trusted that if God was asking me to do this, He would orchestrate it. At the time I extended the invitation, the only commonalities I shared with the women I invited were an interest in Jesus and our daughters' attendance at the same school. I don't know whether I was desperate or naive, but I like to believe that I was leaning in to the Holy Spirit. Since that initial invitation, the moms and daughters in my group, along with their families, have become some of my family's dearest friends. They are our community. The bonus has been that our girls have had a chance to observe, learn, practice, and value the gift of having others in our lives.

Originally I was a bit shocked that these seven women said yes to my invitation; I was not even certain how I was going to lead us! But this has been the story of my life: go, and then God does something profound. For years I had prayed for a group of gals to call my own; I knew that I needed a crew of women to help raise my girls in this harsh world. While my independent spirit made me feel as if I did not want to be tied to such an intense responsibility, my clinical brain knew I needed to commit and press into these relationships, particularly the differences in our wirings, stories, and parenting philosophies. I knew conflicts would eventually arise (though I secretly prayed that we would be exempt from such hardships). On the other hand, my female brain was guarded; I had to fight the fear of letting these women into my life. Now I know we were all afraid, but each of us hosted anticipation and excitement as we banded together.

Because I have two daughters, I wanted each of them to benefit from her own Courageous Girls group. So I led and hosted a Courageous Girls group for each of them. On the first mamas' retreat, I invited both sets of women from the two Courageous Girls groups so that we had twelve women in total. At some point throughout the weekend, *every woman* shared an insecurity with me. It was as though they were making sure I didn't change my mind about the invitation I had extended to them. If we feel this way as moms, we can be sure our girls wrestle with similar feelings.

Many confessed to ways they tried to wiggle out of the retreat just prior to coming. The specific voices in all our heads were different, but the common theme was *I do not belong*. There was the woman who looked put together but felt shame on the inside; the one who felt she was not pretty enough; the one who felt she did not know God or the Bible well enough; the one who shared her childhood abuse and felt deeply afraid to be vulnerable again; the one who knew all the answers but felt alone and really unknown. I heard it all that weekend. I often wish I could bring together all the women I have ever met—in and out of my office—just to say, "You are not alone in your insecurity." Even the well-known and beloved Beth Moore feels it. She really knows Jesus and the truth, and she wrote a whole book on this subject.[8]

One by one I had quiet conversations in ordinary moments with these women. Together we processed the feeling *I do not belong here.* Time and time again, I found myself saying, "You belong here. We all are insecure—even me." (Heads would tilt in curiosity.) I expressed my own feelings to these women: "I have weaknesses I fear you all seeing, but I know in the core of my being that if we trust God, He will use this group to transform us into the women He designed us to be so that our daughters can follow us as we follow Jesus." No one knew the others' insecurities, but as we all sat by a fire and laughed at mama stories that night, we shared our prayer requests. Slowly we realized God was doing something none of us could pinpoint. God was healing each of us with His slow and steadfast ways. He was showing us grace in the flesh. And He still is!

All women are inclined to fight that for which God created us: intimacy with Him and with one another. I tend to blame Eve for this. The garden of Eden was a place where Adam and Eve had full access to be known by and belong to a safe and good God. When the enemy tempted Eve with a simple but crafty distortion of truth ("Did God really say, 'You must not eat from any tree in the garden'?"), you can hear his sarcasm and picture the smirk on his face (Gen. 3:1). When Eve responded, the enemy continued to plant seeds of doubt in her mind: "You will not certainly die.... For God knows that when you eat from it your eyes will be opened, and you will be like God, knowing good and evil" (vv. 4–5). Today the enemy continues to plant thoughts in our minds that God is not who He says He is. Eve had perfect intimacy in the palm of her hand, and she sabotaged it! Can you relate? It seems we question the motives behind people's goodness. *They want something from me. It cannot be pure. There must be a hidden agenda.* Our insecurities rise.

From Eve's first conversation with the serpent, shame entered the garden. It was in that place that we began to hide. The mask (or fig leaves in this case) serves as a false sense of protection or security. Adam and Eve found leaves and covered their nakedness so that they would not feel the shame of vulnerability (see Gen. 3:7). The need to hide ourselves is so powerful, but we fight it. Our girls fight it too. The Bible says that, prior to that moment, Adam and Even were "naked, and they felt no shame" (Gen. 2:25). Imagine what that would have been like! But after Eve ate the fruit, the battle of the sexes began: men started competing and women began scheming out of insecurity. The Genesis account says that when Eve saw the "tree of the knowledge of good and evil," she saw that it was "good for food and pleasing to the eye, and also desirable for gaining wisdom" (2:9; 3:6). I will not go as far as to apply this to every woman, but I do think it's fascinating that Eve was tempted away from pure intimate relationship in the same way many of us use unhealthy coping strategies to find comfort in food, materialism, climbing the ladder, or being knowledgeable about subjects we love.

The American church and the modern lifestyles of our global world have fostered a false sense of community. Somehow the church is buying into it. Even families are divided, busy, and rarely committed to one another. Yet we are designed for so much more. Because of who Jesus is, we can restore what was lost in the garden. Perfectly? No. However, by the power of the Holy Spirit in us and through surrender to Him, we can have moments that resonate with our original design.

We are meant to live a two-pronged approach: one is horizontal and the other is vertical. Similar to how the cross is designed, we are made for horizontal relationships with other human beings and a vertical relationship with an eternal God. Jesus is the center point of it all. We are meant to discover love in both directions as we become more confident in God's love through our identity in Christ and as we grow more secure in loving relationships through the practice of community. Though different, the two approaches are not mutually exclusive. Instead, they intertwine at the center of the cross.

SHE KNOWS AND IS KNOWN BY HER GOD

At the core of a woman who is confident, capable, compassionate, and immersed in healthy community is a well-established identity. She knows who she is, and she knows how to connect well with others. She knows her identity is in what God thinks about her rather than how the world defines her. She knows what God says about her in His Word. Let's examine Psalm 139 and unravel the truths in this passage that counter the messages we hear in society today. Our God is so personal. Take a moment to meditate on this passage, pausing long enough to see which word, phrase, or verse jumps out to you.

> You have searched me, LORD,
>   and you know me.
> You know when I sit and when I rise;
>   you perceive my thoughts from afar.
> You discern my going out and my lying down;
>   you are familiar with all my ways.
> Before a word is on my tongue
>   you, LORD, know it completely.
> You hem me in behind and before,
>   and you lay your hand upon me.
> Such knowledge is too wonderful for me,
>   too lofty for me to attain.
>
> Where can I go from your Spirit?
>   Where can I flee from your presence?

If I go up to the heavens, you are there;
>   if I make my bed in the depths, you are there.
If I rise on the wings of the dawn,
>   if I settle on the far side of the sea,
even there your hand will guide me,
>   your right hand will hold me fast.
If I say, "Surely the darkness will hide me
>   and the light become night around me,"
even the darkness will not be dark to you;
>   the night will shine like the day,
>   for darkness is as light to you.

For you created my inmost being;
>   you knit me together in my mother's womb,
I praise you because I am fearfully and
>   wonderfully made;
>   your works are wonderful,
>   I know that full well.
My frame was not hidden from you
>   when I was made in the secret place.
>   when I was woven together in the depths of
>   the earth.
Your eyes saw my unformed body;
>   all the days ordained for me were written in
>   your book
>   before one of them came to be.
How precious to me are your thoughts, God!
>   How vast is the sum of them!
Were I to count them,
>   they would outnumber the grains of sand—
>   when I awake, I am still with you.

If only you, God, would slay the wicked!
    Away from me, you who are bloodthirsty!
They speak of you with evil intent;
    your adversaries misuse your name.
Do I not hate those who hate you, LORD,
    and abhor those who are in rebellion against you?
I have nothing but hatred for them;
    I count them my enemies.
Search me, God, and know my heart;
    test me and know my anxious thoughts.
See if there is any offensive way in me,
    and lead me in the way everlasting.

HE SEARCHES AND KNOWS ME

Psalm 139 is a powerful place to rest as a believer. There is so much here for us, the daughters of God, to understand. Verse 1 says, "You have searched me, LORD, and you know me." The intimacy of this statement blows me away, for all of us long to be pursued and deeply known. The image of someone searching me may sound invasive or irrelevant. However, every person, male or female, at some point in his or her life wants to be known beyond Sunday morning small talk or polite work conversations. As a therapist, I give this gift to people: to be searched in a safe and noninvasive way that is respectful and in awe of a person's individuality.

Psalm 139 teaches that *because* He searches me, He knows me. The Hebrew word for "know" is *yada* and it has several meanings.[9] One is sharing love sexually, in the same way Adam and Eve *knew* each other to conceive their sons in Genesis 4:1, 25 (ESV). However, another use relates to showing mercy. We see this in other contexts throughout the Bible, such as Proverbs 12:10. The Lord knows you and me intimately—better than we know ourselves! God knows us in ways no one else can or will, and He continues to move toward us. He sees what others may be too busy to see. When no one else in the world seems to understand the depth of our thoughts and feelings, this is a powerful reminder. Even the closest people in our lives—our spouses, our parents, our best friends—do not know us as God does.

Psalm 139 continues by saying that God perceives our thoughts and is familiar with all our ways (see vv. 2–3). The word *familiar* points to the idea that you and I are not strangers to God, even if He seems like one to you. God is like a parent to a child. When our children were born, we knew the sound of their cries. I remember hearing a baby cry in the church nursery, and I could tell the cry belonged to my daughter. I knew her cry among the sounds of other babies. More than that, I was obsessed with figuring out the differences in my daughter's varying cries. Thanks to a random episode of *Oprah*, my husband and I could eventually discern the cries that signaled our baby's various needs: hunger, needing to be changed, tummy troubles, or fatigue. We were so in tune and familiar with our daughter's ways, it became fun to meet her needs and see the relief in both our demeanors when we were able to do so. This is the kind of love God has for us! Becoming a mama helped me understand what it means to be *familiar* with someone.

We do not want to be women who know a lot about God and others while being disconnected from our hearts and bodies. We must avoid being overly cerebral when we read the Word; it *has* to be digested if we want it to change every part of our being and doing. The Word is a love letter to us. And though God is the one who perfectly searches and knows us, He designed us in a way that we still need one another to embody this kind of care in the flesh. God's way of knowing us seems to be most tangible and experiential in the hug of another, a listening ear, a merciful response when we confess, or thoughtful gifts that point to details about us that only those who pay attention would catch. Yet the hope that God intimately captures our hearts better than anyone else can bring us greater healing when our communities are not there in the way we want or need. When we embrace the core truths of Psalm 139, we can risk more with other women because we know we always have a God who understands us when people disappoint.

SHE KNOWS AND IS KNOWN BY OTHERS

Many of our root issues in the counseling room stem from feeling alone. Being able to cope in a harsh world with lots of pain depends on the nature of our care team. The voices in our heads and hearts can steer us toward destructive ways of living if we are left to ourselves. The independent mind-set of *I don't need others* breeds mothers and daughters whose days are based on whatever they feel, think, and experience. That's a risky posture to take and I believe counters everything I read in the Bible. We need to reconsider the plan God had for us originally, which is found in the powerful Greek word for "community": *koinonia*.

In my late teens I was sitting in a classroom with twenty eager young adults from around the country. Our professor gathered us around him in a tight, awkward circle. With direct eye contact and precision in every word, he whispered, "You are Christ's body. All of you are the image of God in the flesh. Together, you are the body of Christ. You are the hands, the feet, the mouth, the ears, the heart … you are Christ to the world."

At that moment I began to understand the necessity of community, not only for our own sense of well-being but for the world to see the power of Christ here and now. I considered myself to be a loving person (you do too; admit it!), but at that moment I realized that the only way love can be reflected is through the dynamic relationships I have with others. Love (apart from God) does not exist in me alone. Love exists *between* you and me.

This powerful truth shaped the next steps of my life as I committed myself to learning to live in intentional community and helping others do the same. Community, though a cliché in many church circles these days, is a lost art in a culture that prides itself on being independent. Though we have swarms of communities gathered online and in the pews Sunday morning, living intentionally with others has become almost vintage, particularly on the West Coast. Maybe in your neck of the woods checking in on neighbors is still the norm, but most have become accustomed to living in silos under the assumption that everyone around us lives as we do. This is far from the truth. One advantage of my career as a therapist has been exposure to the vast variety of stories, cultures, and meanings people live from, both consciously and subconsciously. I am better for it and have come to appreciate God's creative diversity in the body of Christ.

Recently I was reading an article in *Time* magazine about the gender revolution, a sensitive and very present issue today. The article highlighted that we have moved from a binary culture, in which we believed in two genders (male and female), to a culture that has hundreds of expressions of gender and sexuality.[10] Whereas it was once culturally accepted that God determined gender, now each person determines his or her own sense of self. According to shifting cultural norms, we can now choose our child's gender or let the child decide. God no longer decides. A world that has changed the entire definition of gender identity has more of an impact on our daughters than many can or want to imagine.

Within this new paradigm, "me, myself, and I" will determine who I am and who I will be, entirely negating our need to help one another discover our sense of self. We have been told that finding ourselves is a venture we pursue all on our own—apart from our communities. This belief system reinforces the notion that we have the power to change ourselves based on our own feelings and desires. This ideology reestablishes the roots of what the Bible calls our sin nature and causes us to push God aside so that we can live the way we want. Though there seem to be many appealing aspects to the gender revolution, social science and neuroscience tell us something very different. We need one another to discover who we are, and leaving our identity formation to our own discoveries only perpetuates a downward spiral. At the outset it appears that such freedom to choose, even to choose our own gender and sexuality, should bring peace. Rather, statistics tell us that we are more isolated, alone, and depressed than any generation before us. Could these be correlated at all? That might seem overly simplistic, but I beg to ask the question.

Not one of us reflects God fully without another. We need both genders, male and female, to fully reflect the image of God. In the third year of the Courageous Girls curriculum, we dedicate a year to studying how to value our role and contributions within a greater community, as well as how to value others. We often trip over the arrogance that has been fanned by voices saying "You are enough" or "Be who you are" without the caveat that we need community to reflect the fullness of God. The body of Christ, according to God's Word, is made up of male and female, as well as all nations and all tribes—the Gentile and the Jew (see Gal. 3:28). Within that wonderful community lies a wide variety of personalities, gifts, talents, and experiences.

To be known, valued, invited, needed, and honored is a remarkable witness to our independently minded culture. It's hard enough to live this out in our marriages; it's harder still to embrace this among those with whom we have made no promise or covenant. Yet the truth remains that we are better together. Research proves this.

Harvard did a longevity study on how relationships affect our overall health. The *Harvard Gazette* says that a "Harvard study, almost 80 years old, has proved that embracing community helps us live longer, and be happier." As the article's title states, "Good genes are nice, but joy is better."[11] Our joy is made complete when we enter into community and allow the process to sanctify us.

SHE IS HEALED IN RELATIONSHIPS

If we have been wounded in relationships, one of the myths we tell ourselves is that *all we need is God.* Though this is true at its core, our greatest potential takes place in the center of human companionship. As humans, we have common needs to be loved, to dream, and to have purpose in the presence of others. Denying or vilifying these needs can wreak havoc on the soul and in turn cause us to live with masks, guarded hearts, and insecure identities.

Doing life together can start in our homes and extend to others as we grow with fellow mamas and daughters. Remember what Harville Hendrix said: "We are wounded in relationship, and we can be healed in relationship."[12] And even more, we come to know who we are as individuals and our place of belonging within relationships. Ultimately, finding ourselves happens in the context of safe, grace-filled communities, where we are allowed to express a different opinion, share a doubt, or wrestle together with the greater issues in life. Sometimes this requires changing our community experience so that we are exposed to healthier environments. Sometimes this means we are the catalyst to help those around us move beyond surface commonalities to discover greater depths within a community in which God has already sovereignly placed us.

One of my former clients is a pastor and has fully admitted that if it were not for people, he would be a great guy. He struggles with loving people well and is honest about it. He loves theology, teaching the Word, and administering all the details of the church, but the people … well, he could do without them. Loving them has been the hardest work in his ministry. He said all he needed was God, and he wished everyone else would get the same message. Similarly, a woman might join a women's group, hoping to meet her best friend, but she never shares her struggles in the group. Consequently she leaves frustrated, feeling that people did not take the time to get to know her. We all tend to place high expectations on one another, forgetting that God is the only one who can really love us perfectly. The reality of disappointment is a given, but it is not meant to keep us from pressing in. Dietrich Bonhoeffer said it this way: "*Let him who cannot be alone beware of community.… Let him who is not in community beware of being alone.…* Each by itself has profound pitfalls and perils. One who wants fellowship without solitude plunges into the void of words and feelings, and one who seeks solitude without fellowship perishes in the abyss of vanity, self-infatuation, and despair."[13]

No one is exempt from the fragility of human relationships. One of my greatest wounds was in the context of what I thought was a trusted relationship. After we experienced deep betrayal from an entire community, a dear pastor friend checked in on me and my husband. Our entire community had been blindsided by years of deceptions, and I told this pastor that I felt as if I was covered in black tar. I did not know if I could enter back into community with others again after the ripple effect I experienced and watched unfold around me. At the end of our time together, he handed me a Costco-sized hand sanitizer to remind me that God would clean up the tar. He prayed that I would not harden my heart to others. I remember that prayer to this day, as the temptation to walk away from relationships with people in general was real.

Whether we expect too much or too little from people, what we find on the extreme end of the relationship spectrum is a desire to protect ourselves from the fragility of human relationships. We all have internal narratives that keep our walls up: *I need people; I don't need people; I am fine by myself; I should be fine by myself.* Both sides of the coin set us up for unnecessary pain. We were not designed with a need for isolation, nor with the desperation to find our worth in relationships, especially with those who continue to devalue and abuse us. The church at large has promoted the idea that God fulfills all our needs. *Yes, of course He does.* However, He chooses to supply *some* of our needs through people.

SHE CHOOSES HER COMMUNITY WISELY

Choosing our inner circle can make or break the long-term health of community; we need to make our choices wisely. Building relationships with people who can mutually strengthen one another consistently and over time is key. Trust cannot be built quickly, and anyone who claims differently should not be trusted! Brené Brown said, "Trust is a product of vulnerability that grows over time and requires work, attention, and full engagement. Trust isn't a grand gesture—it's a growing marble collection."[14] When we choose *whom* we invest in, as Jesus did with His twelve disciples, we are free to live within our purposes. Choosing does not mean we are free from conflict, but it does mean we participate in it with the Holy Spirit. Christian psychologist Dr. Henry Cloud revolutionized Christians' understanding of healthy relationships when he coauthored the book *Boundaries*. Cloud once said, "Your relationship with God, your relationships with others, and your life practices are going to be the fuel for how you feel, not what is going on around you."[15] Those with whom we choose to spend our time has a far greater impact on our daughters than we know.

Girls today are bombarded with so many false witnesses of community; authentic community is hard to find. When invited to speak on relationships, my husband and I teach that the basic foundation of any healthy relationship is filtered through three questions: *Do I have a voice? Do you have a voice? Am I present?* One's voice represents our individual stories, wirings, needs, thoughts, feelings, and behaviors. Learning how to honor our own voice in any relationship starts with self-awareness. When our natural bent is to focus only on others, dismissing our own voice, codependent tendencies flourish. The church can often subconsciously encourage this kind of imbalance. On the other hand, if we are aware of only our own voice and disregard the voices of others, we travel quickly down the continuum of narcissism.

Creating space to honor both voices in any relationship is crucial to the sustainability of its health. Finally, being present means that we are not distracted by triggers from our past, worries for the future, or sensory overload by our current stressors. The gift of presence is no longer a given in our digitally charged world but rather a skill we have to learn and practice regularly with our daughters. When these three ingredients (my voice, your voice, and being present) are active in relationships, intimacy blossoms. If one ingredient is missing, the relational power is distorted. In this case, we see hints of dysfunction—such as control, manipulation, addiction, or protection—keeping us from experiencing deeper intimacy.

SHE KNOWS HER IDENTITY

Knowing our identity is one thing, but holding on to that truth when others see us differently is something else entirely. Healthy, grace-filled community directs us toward our God-given identity like a compass pointing toward true north. Being rooted in our identity in Christ means we discover what God thinks about us. Many of us never consider His perspective of us and sadly live in communities that forget to point us in that direction. God loves us. Becoming a follower of Christ is a simple decision but is profound and life altering. Knowing our identity in Him lays the foundation for a life of power and purpose. A Courageous Girl believes what God says about her. We need God-aligned, grace-filled communities to remind us of our identity.

I have found that there are thousands of women (and men) who profess Christianity and maybe even attend church regularly but never fully know what God thinks about them according to the Word. At the end of the day, they have no solid relationship with God the Father, Jesus the Son, and the powerful Holy Spirit. These women and girls may end up in our Courageous Girls groups, or this might be you.

As I write about identity in Christ, I want to make sure the entry door to a relationship with God is clear. Imagine a door that serves as the entryway to our lives. God wants to be in our lives, so He will knock at the door to see if He can enter. However, He will never violate our freedom and will, so He will wait at the door until we choose to open it. Some choose not to open the door, but even so He does not stop knocking and He does not leave. He is consistent in His pursuit of relationship with us. When we choose to open the door and invite Him in, He will walk through the door and will commit to be with us in every part of our lives—good, bad, and ugly. In that intimate presence, He allows us to view ourselves through His perspective and plan for us and invites us to venture into a relationship with Him based solely on grace—unearned favor.

In the interest of not veering too far from the main point, I will share only one of the ways the Bible helps us know that Jesus is the way, the truth, and the life (see John 14:6). This concept for most today is hard, because we do not want to leave any other faiths out of the picture. Can I just say that the invitation to have a relationship with God is open to everyone? In fact, *any*one at *any* time can come to God through what Jesus did on the cross and have a thriving relationship with Him. I do not know any other faith system that recognizes the depravity of humanity without requiring us to perform in order to be closer to God.

If you're new to the basics of Christianity or to sharing those basics with others, I invite you to explore the "Romans Road of Salvation" concept found in the book of Romans (see 3:23; 5:8; 6:23; 10:9–10). The outline starts by explaining that we all fall short of the glory of God and can never measure up to His holiness. There is nothing we can do to restore our relationship with God on our own. I think we can all agree that humanity is far from perfect; even when we try to do good, our thoughts and our intentions can be twisted with the desire for selfish gain. Second, the penalty for the relational gap between God and humanity is death, but through Christ, God offers eternal life. The Bible says Christ died while we were still sinners. This means that despite Eve's disobedience in the garden, through the death and resurrection of Christ, life itself is being redeemed. Finally, if you believe in your heart that Jesus died and rose for you personally and if you declare with your mouth that He is Lord of your life, you are both justified and saved.

Justification means we now do not have to earn our way to heaven, but instead we get to receive it! Salvation means God protects us from ourselves and the penalty due us. Both are grace. It can be hard for us to wrap our minds around free gifts; we always think there is a gimmick or ulterior motive. This is never the case with an all-good, all-loving God. He gives freely; all we need to do is open the door of our lives and receive all He has to offer us.

As child development research shows us, all children see themselves through the lens of their parents. Whether we speak to and treat our children with love or with contempt, annoyance, and shame, a parent's perspective and treatment of a child is reflected in the way that child carries himself or herself.[16] Christian parents are not exempt from this. We need an ultimate Parent who helps us see ourselves the way we were created. When we become followers of Jesus, our identity transforms; we become who God says we are. When we accept God as our Father, He can parent us in a way that helps us assess how we see ourselves and reconstruct that image in the light. You are defined by your belonging: when you accept God the Father as your ultimate Parent, you affirm your belonging to His family and your identity as a saint. When you know who and whose you are, you know you have been made with purpose and equipped with courage to fulfill your God-given destiny.

Mamas, we are called to raise our daughters to know who and whose they are so that they can be courageous. It starts with our own relationship with God and how we link arms with others. Before you move on to the next chapter, take a moment to read a few of the verses from the Takeaway exercise and let them wash over your mind, heart, and body. This is not an exhaustive list, believe me. You may not believe these yet, but that is okay. Trust the process. Remember, discovering who we are takes practice in the confines of grace-based community, where being known breathes life and meaning beyond our imagination.

Takeaway

Pick three to five verses about identity in Christ and choose to memorize them. You will find a list of Scriptures in the back of the book. These verses will help you discern who in your community helps you move toward truth. Identify a Scripture that is hard to accept, and ask God and another person in your community to help you grow in believing this truth. Give the list to your daughter, and have her choose one or two Scriptures she wants to memorize as well. Ask her which Scripture is harder for her to believe, and pray with her routinely about this struggle until you both recognize the difference in her spirit. As a challenge, attempt to memorize Psalm 139 with your daughter. Write it on a piece of paper, and put it in a place where you will see it daily, like the bathroom mirror or the refrigerator. When we have God's Word embedded in our hearts, we can steer our daughters, ourselves, and our communities back to what He says about us.

Take It a Step Further

Does your community bring you back to your identity in Christ? Journal about a time when you felt safe, known, and seen in the context of relationships. Then write about a time when you felt unsafe. Take one practical step toward engaging in community and inviting people into your life. The first step is saying yes to the invitation from God.

6

She Makes and Keeps Friends

It always helps to have people we love beside us when we have
to do difficult things in life.... As human beings, our job in
life is to help people realize how rare and valuable each one
of us really is, that each of us has something that no one else
has—or ever will have—something inside that is unique to
all time. It's our job to encourage each other to discover that
uniqueness and to provide ways of developing its expression.

Fred Rogers, *The World According to Mister Rogers*

Teaching a Courageous Girl how to be a good friend can be as difficult as teaching her how to fly. It's more complicated than we ever
imagined and requires delicate training. As we interact with the
different phases of our daughters' social lives, every wound in us
regarding friendship seems to reopen. Wiring, circumstances, and
coaching all play a role in how our daughters develop their sense of
value, confidence, and safety within friendships. Some of us try to

control friendships; others of us try to avoid them. Most of us are desperately praying about them.

SHE INITIATES

I don't know about you, but I always have had to pray for friends. I remember moving many times as a girl; I would ask for a Christian friend at each location. God provided every time, in every move and in every situation. He did not always provide these female friends according to my timetable, but His provision never ceased to amaze me. So if you want good friends for you and your daughter, first pray.

Second, if you want to have good friends, you need to be a good friend. If you wish others would extend an invitation, be the first to invite. Scottish pastor Alistair Begg once said, "The love of God is an initiative-taking love; in fact, genuine love always takes the initiative."[1] Though this feels intimidating and may trigger our fears of rejection and pride, this is the reality of where friendship begins. Someone needs to initiate. If you want to be friends with someone, I would challenge you to believe that God is asking you to take a step forward in faith.

Waiting for others to move can be agonizing and cause us to feel powerless. But inviting someone to coffee or organizing a playdate shifts the power. As adults, we might feel vulnerable when initiating invitations; little girls start out having it a little easier. They begin with an innocent ideal that when you ask a friend to play, that friend will say yes. And if that friend says no, you simply play with another friend. Sometime in elementary school, this changes. Girls start to acquire the same thinking as us adults, creating cliques to divide who is "in" from who is "out." Being able to help our daughters navigate the world of friendship requires us to understand our own beliefs, biases, and experiences about having friends. This is important so that we do not model out of our own wounds but instead out of what God has purposed for us all.

What we model in our adult friendships always speaks louder to our daughters than what we preach. Because of our unique wirings and our histories, we approach making friends differently. Having grace for our own hesitancies allows us to be patient with ourselves and our daughters. Alongside your daughter, learn how to be a good friend. Identify if you are a natural people person or prefer a quieter day reading by yourself. Introverts, those who need more alone time, still need friends but prefer one-to-one or smaller groups. More extroverted people, those who like processing with others, enjoy meeting new people and having an extended network of friends. Think about your history of friendships and which relationships felt the most safe, healthy, and life giving. Consider how those friendships developed and why they felt the most fruitful in your life. Ask why the friendship ended—because the seasons changed or because there was unresolved conflict? Then begin to pray about whom to start practicing with in your own community. Starting or joining a Courageous Girls group can be a natural step to practice developing healthier friendships for both you and your daughter. Finding trusting and lasting friendships requires action beyond what many of us want or are willing to do, but our daughters need to see the process in our lives if they're going to have sustainable friendships in theirs.

SHE REFUSES THE LIES WE TELL OURSELVES

There are subtle lies we, as women, tell ourselves and sometimes even speak out loud that keep us paralyzed. These lies seep into the paradigms our daughters hold and keep up the walls that we are desperate to see fall. We might tell ourselves or others, "If she wanted to hang out with me, she would invite me to hang out." Or perhaps we might believe that "I am not valuable or worthy to be chosen as a friend." Maybe you have felt used in friendships and called on only when needed for a resource or expertise. Maybe you have never had a friend whom you could trust with your deepest hurt. Maybe hanging out for the sake of relationships feels pointless or odd in some way. Many things keep us from moving toward one another.

As a girl who moved many times during childhood, I know what it is like to start over. When my family moved from Arizona to Washington state, I changed cultures, said good-bye to one of my best friends, and kissed the sun adios. The city of Puyallup welcomed me with ninety straight days of rain in a record-setting year. It was not an easy transition. Moving too many times as a child can be traumatic for many people. But in my case, it built a skill set for which I have become thankful in my adult life. While there were many seasons of feeling unknown and trying to find some sense of belonging, being the new girl often meant I became popular quickly. However, that popularity did not translate to having deep friendships until I made a decision to pursue others.

I learned early on that, at some level, everyone is guarded and cautious about making a new friend. The way we perceive one another can be the greatest barrier. For example, I have a dear friend who is extremely introverted and gives off the impression that she is mad or arrogant. In reality, she is the gentlest and kindest woman I know, but her face tells another story. Learning and teaching our girls the power of body language is a good place to start when teaching about friendship. Remembering to smile, making eye contact, and asking good questions are all simple ways we build connections with others. Finding the courage to initiate a conversation with someone we want to know better may be the only path to friendship with that person. One of my lifelong friends approached me on the first day of high school. Sporting her black high-tops, she extended an invitation to her birthday party, where I was welcomed into a group of girls I would have otherwise not known. I challenge you—be the first to extend the invitation. Yes, girls and women can be mean, but in many cases they are just insecure and cautious. If you initiate, you might find your best friend and a few other Courageous Mamas to journey alongside. If we can learn this lesson ourselves, we will be better prepared to coach our daughters when they find themselves in similar situations.

As I mentioned earlier, I barely knew any of the women I invited to join my first Courageous Girls group in 2012. Now these women have become my closest tribe of friends. I prayed for a group of women to travel with through motherhood, and God answered. I am grateful they said yes to my crazy invitation. This was not easy for me, but many years of being the new girl gave me the courage to extend invitations to friendship as an adult. So many moms are waiting to be invited into community. If you have yet to find your tribe, start praying!

SHE HONORS HERSELF AND OTHERS

God has created a wide variety of people, and I happen to be someone who finds joy in that diversity. Learning what makes us unique helps us draw out others and honor their contributions in relationships. Conflict often occurs because of misunderstandings, rather than actual sin and intentional wrongdoings. God has created a variety of people to reflect the greatness of who we are and the depth of who He is.

My husband and I have used many personality assessments throughout our years in ministry, leadership development, and counseling. Our favorite has become the Core Values Index (CVI) created by Lynn E. Taylor, president of Taylor Protocols in Seattle.[2] This instrument has an astounding 97 percent retest reliability. This means that if you take this assessment every two years for the rest of your life, you will find only a 3 percent shift. Taylor's motivation for creating the tool came from his belief that if you show people who they really are, then they will do something meaningful with their lives.

The CVI explains a variety of ways we are motivated, communicate, learn, and handle conflict. Using the terms *Merchant, Builder, Innovator,* and *Banker,* the assessment reveals how much of each hard-wiring archetype we have within us. Knowing the amount of each core value that God knit in us helps us understand our unique fingerprint. Though the assessment was not created with this in mind, my husband and I think all four core values reflect the image of God. Each person has parts of God's character to varying degrees. Our lack in one area points us to the fact that we need one another to be the body of Christ. One is not better or greater than another; instead, we complement one another.

In the assessment each core value ranges from a low of zero to a high of thirty-six. The higher the number, the more intensely a core value is expressed in a person's life. Part of the genius of this instrument is learning what motivates, what creates anxiety and conflict, and how we can choose to shift from one core value to another based on what is needed in different environments and relationships. This becomes a powerful tool for mother-daughter relationships and for the development of healthy Courageous Girls groups. Here is a brief overview of each core value, which is explored purposely throughout the Courageous Girls years.

Merchants are highly relational individuals who live out of truth and love. For Merchants, truth is the ability to see things the way they are, and love is the ability to honor the core values in oneself and in others. Merchants are visionaries and love to encourage those around them. They think about how their relationships are affected as they move through life. Merchants love to communicate and feel their way through the world. They have X-ray vision for people's emotions. They learn and communicate through verbal processing with other human beings. Without the Merchants, we would miss the need to connect and celebrate. Merchants love nothing better than a party to celebrate others or a reason to cast vision beyond what others believe possible.

Builders are task-oriented people who live out of power and faith. Their power is used to make a positive difference, and their faith is the ability to know what to do. They do not want or need to read the instruction manual when trying something new. They have an intense need to close the deal and finish a task, and they love to encourage others to do the same. They are the action- and results-oriented members of the community; they learn by doing. They communicate with a few intentional words. Without the Builders, the rest of us would talk or think our way through life without ever acting on our words and ideas.

Innovators are systems thinkers who live out of wisdom and compassion. Their wisdom is the ability to both see the way things are and to know what to do about it, and their compassion is the capacity to remain inquisitive until all the data is collected. These are the wise sages of the group who can often think outside the box and hold messy, complex problems well. They can be taken advantage of because they are the problem solvers in the community. They may find themselves having a hard time saying no because of their steadfast compassion. They learn by assessing solutions in their minds and communicate complex thoughts. Without them, the community might do the same thing over and over without getting new results. As their name indicates, this group finds joy in innovating and creating new solutions for the community.

Bankers are fact-driven people who live out of knowledge and justice. They love to be organized, practice precision, and gather the facts. "Meet at twelve o'clock in the afternoon" means "arrive sharply at noon." They tend not to speak unless they are certain of what they are sharing. They are thoughtful, as they remember details about others that the rest of the community misses. These people care about equity in the community and will notice when others are missing resources or are being treated unfairly. They learn by reading information and communicate with others by giving detailed, linear data after being sure of what they have to say. Without the Banker's black-and-white meter detecting right from wrong, we would miss out on order, precision, and justice.

When we can notice others and the way they bring value to our communities, something profound occurs: kingdom living. So often as moms we are tempted to raise our daughters to be like us, but seeing a daughter's unique wiring can help us know how to partner well with her and assess where conflicts might arise, as well as help her build confidence in her own God-given contributions to the world. This is where knowledge can equip us to fan the flame of our daughter's gifts and prevent us from overshadowing her sense of self. This can give us great direction on how to parent as well as show grace.

For example, my oldest daughter and I are different in a few key core values. We talk about this openly and have found ways to navigate her frustrations with my lack of attention to detail. Similarly, I have grown in ways that encourage her ability to cue in to the details. Rather than moving into the "you do not understand me" phase, she knows that I am trying to honor her Banker value by giving her the ability to research our family vacations, organize Courageous Girls gatherings, and share the many facts she learns as she reads and absorbs information at school. My hope is that all our girls will not only leave our homes feeling ready and equipped to be whom God made them but will also be so self-confident they won't compare themselves with siblings or other girls. Rather, they will see one another as partners, not as competition, in the greater work God is doing. We need every core value—the people person, the task person, the idea person, and the detail person—in order to reflect the glory of God.

The comparison game comes from a place of insecurity—not knowing who we are and wanting to be like someone else. It's a normal but deadly trap that sucks energy never intended to be spent in such a way. In fact, the CVI tells us that when we are trying to live out of the core values in which we score lower, we not only are causing greater emotional and mental angst but also are cutting the world short of our greatest contributions to the wider community. God did not design us to drift slowly from our hard wiring and God-given design. Instead, we are to embrace our strengths and our limitations as a way to give and receive in community. Friendships are a way to partner together to face life's hardships—like illness, job losses, death, family difficulties. And yes, even when our children are struggling, friendships are meant to provide the support, prayer, and encouragement we need to walk them through their own difficult moments.

Often friendships are formed but fade fast over small misunderstandings or differences. Many times these differences are simply related to how people are wired; different wirings have different communication styles. Sometimes we are (figuratively) speaking a different language and do not even know it. If we learn to name the ways we are similar and different, we will begin to honor ourselves and others. In this process, we will transform our approach to building relationships and communicating with others and will create longevity in our friendships.

SHE IS COMMITTED THROUGH THE CONFLICTS

The Bible is clear that finding a friend is like finding a ruby. So keeping a good friend is worth it! Proverbs 20:6 says, "Many will say they are loyal friends, but who can find one who is truly reliable?" (NLT). It may not seem encouraging at first, but I find this verse helpful because it validates the difficulty of finding and keeping good friends. It might be easy for some to make friends, but it takes great character and integrity to keep them. If you are friends with anyone long enough and if you are really going deep in your relationship, conflict is bound to happen. If you do not experience any conflict, then your relationship is still treading water and has not ventured into the deep end of the pool yet. A long time ago, I decided that in order to teach my girls how to be friends and keep friends, I would have to learn to do the same. That means moving through conflict rather than around it. The natural people-pleaser in me would rather smile and stuff my feelings of hurt, but I have been a therapist long enough to know that is not a viable way forward.

Dealing with conflict can feel like extra work and unwanted drama for many of us. However, our unhealthy coping patterns can take more effort than healthy ones. In fact, if we dig further into the CVI, we learn that each wiring has its own style of conflict, each of which is poisonous to healthy relationships: the Merchant will manipulate; the Builder will intimidate; the Innovator will interrogate; and the Banker will become aloof in judgment. (This is covered in year 5 of the Courageous Girls curriculum.) These conflict strategies arise whenever we feel as if our core values are not honored by another. These responses to conflict look different depending on a person's unique wiring. However, in all cases, the energy it takes to live out of our conflict strategies—rather than trying to approach conflict in a healthy manner—moves us into isolation and further from meeting our truest needs of restoration and intimacy.

It takes energy to ignore someone, employ passive aggression, withdraw our love, blow up in anger, gossip, build alliances, defend our case, or pretend as if everything is okay. The anger, guilt, and resentment we carry under the surface can be just as destructive as saying the wrong thing or being rejected. Conflict isn't always negative or unproductive; in fact, many research studies have shown that the quantity of conflict in a relationship is not as important as how the conflict is handled. When conflict is managed well, it has the potential to lead to more satisfactory relationships.[3] Even God would rather us come to Him with our doubts, hurts, concerns, and fears—and wrestle honestly with Him—than remain distant for the sake of keeping the peace.

Conflict is a necessary ingredient in the process of being known and building intimacy. Without it, relationships remain shallow and one will never know whether they can be trusted in a storm. The essence of our faith is rooted in a narrative that moves through conflict. Dr. John Gottman, a marriage expert in the clinical world, ran a relationship lab in Seattle where he watched couples interacting. After almost forty years, he consistently found that the number one predicting factor in whether or not a relationship would last is how the couple handles conflict. He says he can predict whether a marriage will survive at 91 percent accuracy![4] Since our children learn relationship skills in the home they grow up in, moms (and dads) are the key teachers in this area.

The next logical connection is that in order to mother Courageous Girls well, we must learn how to fight fairly ourselves. Conflict becomes toxic only when it is ignored and unresolved. It begins to ferment in our souls and create side effects. There is a direct correlation between the health of a relationship and how quickly the people in that relationship repair their hurts. This means that once you have wounded each other, which happens in every human relationship sustained over time, the length of time it takes to work through the hurt directly reflects the relationship's health and sustainability. Fighting fairly means that we play by the rules and leave out what Dr. Gottman called "the Four Horsemen of the Apocalypse"—criticism, contempt, defensiveness, and stonewalling.[5]

Instead, we should use healthy communication so that both parties can be heard and understood, taking any actions needed to make amends so that we can draw closer to God and each other.

These principles are powerful ones, *and* they align perfectly with God's Word. This is my favorite part of research! It continues to improve each year, proving the wisdom of God and the practicality of the Bible. Dr. Gottman said that "a repair attempt," the attempt to get a relationship back on track, is a secret weapon of emotionally intelligent people. He said that a repair attempt is "any statement or action—silly or otherwise—that prevents negativity from escalating out of control."[6] Every other relationship expert, including the Lord, would agree that trying to move toward someone rather than away from that person is a healthier starting point.

One of my favorite parts of the Christian faith is that we are not asked to be perfect and that we have a remedy for when we mess up—the help of the Holy Spirit. Though some believe that Matthew 5:48—"Be perfect, therefore, as your heavenly Father is perfect"— means that Christians should have no sign of sin, this kind of thinking keeps us from maturing in our faith journey and leaning in to the transformational power of Christ. Simply, it alludes to the idea that if you are not perfect, then you are not a follower of Jesus. In reality, the more mature we are in our faith journey, the more aware we are of our sin nature. We are slower to react to others and therefore press deeper into the strength of the Holy Spirit and the wisdom of the Word. The more we mature in our faith journeys, the quicker we are to recognize our own limitations and accept the power of God working through our weaknesses.[7] As the leaders of the ministry Trueface put it, we come out of hiding and begin to face the reality of our condition with God and others.[8] This is a lifelong process, and we know we will be made complete when we see Jesus face to face in heaven. I pray our Courageous Girls capture this message of grace because it's the context in which we maneuver through our friendships. This way of thinking helps us see a key difference between being human and sinning, though both can create conflict. When they do, both require moving through *repair* with those around us.

This last summer, on a leisurely Saturday afternoon, I decided to go shopping with my daughters. The three of us joyfully jumped in the car, and I, as usual, drove my car out of our garage, maneuvering in my typical manner up our gravel driveway toward the road. As I turned to leave our country home, I heard a *bang*! To my utter surprise, I hit our friend's parked car *right outside my home*. I was in a car accident in my own front yard! No one was hurt, but my girls watched me lean my head against the steering wheel to pray out loud. (I did not start singing Carrie Underwood, but I sure felt the need to have Jesus take the wheel.)

Before I could get out of the car, my husband, Jeff, and our dear friend (the car's owner) came to check on us. I could see by Jeff's face that he was trying to make a split-second decision: either to be mad at me for such a clumsy move or to have compassion for me as he saw my embarrassment and remorse. If I had looked in my rearview mirror before exiting the garage, I could have avoided the situation. But no … not this time.

As my daughters watched the drama unfold, they learned many lessons. Instead of being met with anger, I was met with comfort and concern. Our friend's car was quite damaged in the collision, and Jeff and I both assured him we would make it right on our end. After a brief assessment, we all went our own way: the girls and I went shopping and the men continued to hang out. Immediately, insecurity set in. I thought of my friend and his wife, both Bankers in the CVI index: careful and thoughtful people with a potential for aloof judgment. My core values began to emerge: the Merchant inside me wanted to cry; my Innovator wanted to blame the situation on our friend for choosing to park where he did. (Even though he used the same spot everyone uses when visiting our home!) Wanting to feel the shame of my careless move, an internal voice communicated that no one else had ever done something like this. Then panic set in as I considered that my mistake could cause my friends to judge me, mistrust me, and possibly keep their distance from me.

Before my daughters and I had reached our destination, my husband and our friend's wife (one of my Courageous Girls mamas) left me separate voice-mail messages that I played out loud to my girls. Careful and thoughtful, each of them wanted to communicate they understood that what I had done was simply a mistake. They added that they were praying the mishap would not ruin what my daughters and I had set out to do that afternoon. Their concern was moving, and I shared with the girls that both people could have responded very differently to my actions. However, in their grace for me, I was set free to be fully present with my daughters. I texted Jeff, saying, "Because my identity in Christ is rooted in what God thinks of me, I am free to own this mistake and make it right. I own every part of hitting our friend's car and am grateful for the grace he showed me. This is a sober reminder that the ever-clumsy and fast-moving Terra still remains after forty years of trying to slow down!—in every sense of the words. Thank God for these reminders and to know I am loved in the midst of something that could cause guilt, shame, and a ripple effect of other poor behaviors."

I have taught conflict-resolution skills for years to every kind of person. It seems that those whose identity is rooted in Christ have an easier time moving through the heat. Being rooted simply means that I know who I am because of what God says about me and that my circumstances, choices, or others' opinions do not dictate my value or worth. After my accident I could have held the guilt of hitting our friend's car for days, months, years. However, Christ says I am loved, forgiven, redeemed, and a work in process that He will finish. Knowing these identity statements frees me to be human and know what to do when I mess up. Remember what Dr. Landreth and other experts said, "What's most important may not be what you do, but what you do after what you did!"[9]

Because I know I am loved, I can (1) own my choices and mistakes; (2) recognize the consequences I caused the other person; (3) empathize with that person's pain; (4) ask for forgiveness; and (5) make it right, if I can. In my situation, making it right meant starting an insurance claim on our end and confirming that our friend's car was cared for as soon as possible. I could not go back in time, but I could make sure I learned from my mistake. (In case you were wondering, I drive very slowly out of my garage now.)

If I find my identity only in what I do, then moving beyond my mistakes can turn into lingering shame, defensiveness, blame, minimizing damage, denial, and more. For some, even the act of making things right leaves lingering guilt and a desire to hide. We need to remember that this kind of conflict happens all the time and that if we react poorly, it can lead to bondage and relationship ruin. If we learn to handle conflict well, our children will benefit from our mistakes. I saw the car accident as a teaching moment, and I tried to help my daughters process what they saw at the first opportunity.

I even explained how Daddy and I would make it right and admitted out loud, "What happened was my fault." I pointed out the difference between how our friend could have responded and how he actually responded. I pointed out that I was given grace, patience, and gentleness and that I was grateful for it. The conversation was better than I could have expected, and I appreciated the chance to impart a real-life lesson.

The word *conflict* means "to come into collision or disagreement; be contradictory, at variance, or in opposition; clash."[10] Despite a few personalities who delight in debating, most people prefer harmony and would rather dismiss their own voices for the sake of keeping peace. In fact, many Christian cultures teach this kind of thinking: it is better to have peace than to make your own voice heard. I believe this concept confuses the idea of humility with codependency and passivity.

Humility, in its purest definition, is having a sober mind-set about ourselves. We are neither better nor worse than any other. Philippians 2 tells us that Jesus modeled humility as He left His throne of glory and humbled Himself to become a baby boy, entering our world and choosing to restrain His power. Jesus was not less than us. Instead, His humility was in His choice to submit, out of love, to God the Father and to join us in our human existence. I have come to understand *submission* as a love word rather than a powerless word. As females in the church, we are cultured to be sweet and quiet. Beyond church culture, an outspoken woman maybe be applauded or seen as aggressive. It seems culture places women on a pendulum swing between staying silent and needing to scream. However, Jesus' model of humility is for both males and females. Jesus did not take a passive role, but rather He took an assertive "on mission" role that makes choices out of love, purpose, and grace.

When you know who you are, you do not need to convince others of who you are; this is humility. If we become comfortable with who we are, we will speak truth to one another. Our mere backgrounds, wirings, and broken humanity will create moments of potential collision. Proverbs 27:5–6, 17 says it beautifully: "Better is open rebuke than hidden love. Wounds from a friend can be trusted, but an enemy multiplies kisses.... As iron sharpens iron, so one person sharpens another." A faithful friend will move through conflict with you and will not offer you fake kisses or hidden love. She will speak to you with truth and will trust you with her heart. She will tell you when she was offended and needs repair. She will own her mistakes, and instead of defending them, she will try to make them right. She will empathize with your perspective and learn how to serve you even if it's different from her way. She will not avoid you, but she will pray and trust that God will show her how to make amends. Courageous is the woman who is committed through conflict and humble enough to honor her own needs alongside the needs of others.

SHE HAS BOUNDARIES: RED LIGHT, YELLOW LIGHT, GREEN LIGHT

Many are confused by how to move through conflict, especially when it's time to set a boundary with a hurtful person who has sinned again them repeatedly. Confusing messages, often meant with good intentions, have left many women and girls uncertain of how to discern when it's time to close a door on a friendship or continue trying for repair. Not all friends will remain close friends, even safe friends, and the Bible is clear about this. Matthew 18 is dedicated to addressing people who continue to wrong us and is unwilling to own their mistakes or turn away from their hurtful ways (see vv. 15–17). Through time and conflicts, we learn whether a friend is a red-, yellow-, or green-light friend. The Courageous Girls curriculum provides help for processing this issue in various ways at each age level since it is such a vital part of being a Courageous Girl. Using the analogy of a traffic light that gives clear direction to vehicles on the road, we can see three types of relationships we need to consider as moms raising daughters.

Red-light people are those who do not respect our boundaries, and even when we have asked for change, they dismiss our voices, continuing on as if their needs are the only ones that matter. These red-light people are considered unsafe; it would be enabling to maintain a relationship with them or ask our daughters to do the same. Red-light people are those who do harm to others and have no remorse or changed behaviors. They may even say they are sorry, but their actions will reveal whether or not they are truly repentant. Repentance means to make a 180-degree turn and move in the opposite direction. Those whose words cannot be trusted and who continue harming people can be what the Bible calls wolves in sheep's clothing: they delight in doing wrong and are unwilling to change. The color red, like in a traffic light, symbolizes the need to stop the relationship altogether until there is evidence of full repentance over an extended period of time (two-plus years is a safe reference point in these cases). Red-light people will not understand and will likely make you out to be the bad guy. Boundaries in these cases will need to remain high. The application of this principle must be used wisely, prayerfully, and with great counsel.

Yellow-light people are hot and cold. Some days they respond to your needs, and other days they talk about you behind your back. They might not harm you or others on purpose, but they are people whom the Bible calls fools because they blame the circumstances around them rather than owning their participation in the problem. These friends are repentant at times and may not overtly try to hurt us, but they are inconsistent and cannot be fully trusted. Similar to a yellow light in traffic, we slow down and are cautious with these friends. We are kind, respectful, and often associate with these people still. However, we do not let these people into our trusted inner circle unless they show healthy movement toward becoming a green-light person.

Green-light people are friends who make mistakes and have bad days, but they are always willing to own their behaviors and make things right. Their intent is never to harm you. These friends may go through hard seasons and may not always be the best of friends, but that is when you get to serve them and be the friend they need. The tides will change, and one day you will have your turn. Green-light friends are trustworthy; they speak truth, work through conflicts, and move toward forgiveness. We can see repentance in their changed behaviors, and they follow through on what they say. The Bible calls these people wise. They are not perfect, but they demonstrate hearts that want to remain in a right relationship with you and God.[11]

SHE CONFESSES AND FORGIVES

Ruth Haley Barton once said, "One thing we can know for sure is that when we are confessing our sin to God but not to the people around us in ordinary, nitty-gritty life, there is not much real spiritual transformation going on."[12] When we are in courage and surrounded by a community of moms who allow us to be ourselves authentically, then we can confess to one another the hidden places of our hearts and souls. Confession is not always the expression of something we did wrong but can be the confession of all of who we are: our dreams, hopes, and shortcomings. Have you told anyone your childhood story? Have you ever shared your greatest fears or the shame voices you hear in your head? James 5:16 says, "Confess your sins to each other and pray for each other so that you may be healed. The prayer of a righteous person is powerful and effective." Transformation and healing can occur when we open our mouths and tell one another what is really going on inside us. Friends who are willing not only to listen but also to safely acknowledge our struggle and pray for us, rather than judge or try to fix us, are the kind who bring healing. Some of the latest research has shown us that our brains are repairing themselves as we empathize with one another.[13] I wonder if that is why God asks us to confess to one another.

Telling another human being what we can own in our own lives is just as courageous as forgiving someone who has wronged us. Forgiveness is more profound than most of us realize. It is not the absence of caring, nor is it merely brushing things off. In fact, it is quite the opposite. We often say trite things like "Forgive and forget" or "Forgive as God has forgiven you." However, these statements do not fully embrace the extended facets of forgiveness. God does not forget; He chooses not to remember. That is the difference between a willful choice and a momentary absence of mind.

The Greek word used for "forgive" is *aphiēmi*, meaning "to let go."[14] In order to forgive, we need to know what we are letting go. A simple way to forgive that honors both the heart and the profound nature of what forgiveness is meant to be follows these steps. First, name the offense, recognizing its consequences and how it made you feel. Then grieve. Depending on the offense, the grief will have different lengths of time. Then choose to let the offense go into the hands of a just God. Many of us need to be reminded of the ways God is just in order to hand over the pain of another's sin against us, whether known or unknown. We need to truly wrestle with and hold tight to how our righteous God is both merciful *and* faithful to meet the evils of this world with a right response. As we read through Scripture, we find that His justice is not always aligned with our idea of it, but He is surely a God who sees and will make all things right someday. This process is not the only way to forgive, but for me it has become the way that feels the most concrete and transformative in my life and others'. It is important to note that the choice to forgive is actually one of the last steps in any healing process, though Christians often suggest it is the first.

Jesus journeyed through the garden of Gethsemane, feeling the weight of His choice to forgive, before He gave His life on the cross. As I work with survivors of sexual abuse and sexual betrayal, the notion of forgiving before grieving not only feels like retraumatizing a survivor but also seems entirely unbalanced. Choosing to forgive often requires a clear sense of boundaries and a healthy restoration of a person's power to choose. *Mending the Soul* by Steve and Celestia Tracy, a beautifully crafted biblical and trauma-informed recovery book and workbook, helps unravel the complexity of forgiveness and why it is okay to take time to forgive as well as refrain from restoring relationships with unrepentant red-light people.[15]

Courageous Girls understand that forgiveness is not just a word we flippantly throw around but a transformational process that helps us stay aligned with God and others. The steps of moving through forgiveness allow our full person to move forward: soul, brain, mind, heart, and body. We help our daughters disrupt cycles of abuse and value their worth as women. Telling a daughter to forgive an abusive person[16] before protection occurs only puts her in the way of continued harm. The process of naming and feeling the emotions associated with the offense—and then choosing not to punish someone for what that person has done—allows God to do as He sees fit. He will offer the abuser either mercy or justice, but the point is that it's His decision. Forgiveness does not equal trust or relationship restoration. We can forgive *and* keep our boundaries in place with those who are unrepentant and unsafe. This brings a small amount of comfort in the face of all the awful abuse humanity has experienced.

Most of the time, we are not forgiving abusive dynamics, but rather we're forgiving miscommunications and clumsy collisions. There are times when this forgiveness process must take place between me and God. I take this opportunity to pray the forgiveness process out loud or write it in my journal as a letter to Him. I can do this even when I do not have a relationship with a person any longer. In healthier relationships I can take the grievance directly to my friend. Matthew 18:15 says that if your brother or sister has sinned, go and point out his or her offense. Matthew 5:23–24 says that if you remember that your brother or sister has something against you, go to him or her before you bring your gift to the altar. In either case, you are to go and confront the person, not wait until he or she magically recalls offending you. Expecting someone to know he or she hurt or offended you is not a realistic expectation. This is called *mind reading*, and I am not sure I have met anyone who does it well. Often we do not know we have hurt someone until we are told. But if our relationship is a green one, then we will work through the conflict with confession and forgiveness until we are right with each other again.

I will leave you with a few final reminders that help us moms navigate our relationships in ways that teach our daughters to as well. Forgiveness is not equated with trust. Trust is built over time and consistent actions with repentant hearts. In order for a relationship to be reconciled, forgiveness must happen. However, forgiveness can happen without reconciliation. Reconciliation requires two parties who are willing to own and change behaviors in order to rebuild trust. Recalling the hurt from our relationships with others can be a reminder of how God has faithfully rescued you and given you wisdom and discernment for present relationships. Forgiveness is a process that recognizes the gravity of harm done and, in doing so, helps us honor our own emotions, mind-set, and experiences for deeper healing and lasting change.

Working through conflict and learning to forgive are the final ingredients of a healthy, quality friendship. No true friend is made overnight; friendship takes slow and steady investment, intention, and conflict management. Making friends can be the first hurdle, but keeping them is where Courageous Girls find the depths of God's heart for His church. This is where we all grow as children of God and experience intimacy as we become vulnerable, real, and honest with one another. A girl who has one to three friends who will go the distance with her is truly rich. As the Word says, who is really faithful? (see Prov. 20:6). A Courageous Mama and her daughter can be faithful because of who Jesus is and what He does in and through us as we allow Him to lead the way.

Takeaway

Make a list of the women in your life. See if you can discern prayerfully who is a red-, yellow-, or green-light friend. If you need to set some boundaries with your red- and yellow-light friends, write down one or two boundaries you will put into action this week. Tell your green-light friends how grateful you are to have them in your life. Write them a card or send them a text to remind them of their role in your life. If boundaries are hard for you, consider reading the book *Boundaries* by Dr. Townsend and Dr. Cloud. If you do not have any good friends you can name, prayerfully ask God to bring them into your life. If God brings anyone to mind, initiate a coffee date!

Take It a Step Further

If you need to work through unforgiveness, start by writing down the names of people who have hurt you and what they have done. Write down how each offense has made you feel, and list any consequences that have occurred since the offense took place. Ask the Lord if you are to go and talk to your friend or work through your forgiveness with Him. In either case, identify if this hurt results from a personality conflict or a sinful behavior. Finally, consider any way you have contributed to the hurt. You may be completely innocent, but Matthew 7:3–5 reminds us that before we go to people about how they have wronged us, we need to make sure we have assessed our own hearts and can approach them with gentleness.

Second, practice asking your daughter for forgiveness anytime she tells you about a hurt you caused her. If she tells you that you have hurt her, that is a huge step forward for your relationship! It means you are safe for her to be honest. Practice saying the words "Will you forgive me?" Invite her to participate in the forgiveness process by offering you the words "Yes, I choose to forgive you" or "I need some time, Mom." Both responses are okay. Each wiring needs different things for closure. The Merchant needs to see emotional remorse. The Builder needs direct ownership with no excuses. The Banker needs time and wants to see you make it right. The Innovator needs to understand the context and reasons behind the behavior. Remember to tell your daughter how you will intentionally make it right. This pattern will help you both learn how to practice forgiveness with friends in and outside your Courageous Girls group.[17]

7

She Is Fearless ... Almost

Being brave isn't the absence of fear.
Being brave is having that fear
but finding a way through it.
Bear Grylls

I have learned over the years that when one's
mind is made up, this diminishes fear; knowing
what must be done does away with fear.
Rosa Parks, *Quiet Strength*

When I think about what I want for our daughters, I think of freedom from fear. By *fear*, I mean the kind that causes us to live limited lives: fear of doing what God is asking of us, fear of being ourselves, fear of ruining our daughters, fear of messing up, fear of success, fear of the world, and so forth. God longs to help us and our girls move through these kinds of fears, asking us to replace them with something far more powerful: faith.

SHE FEEDS HER FAITH, NOT HER FEARS

There is a pillow in my living room that reads, "Let your faith be bigger than your fears." I am always reminded of Queen Esther, an ordinary woman with wounds of her own who was used in extraordinary circumstances. Esther was a beautiful young virgin in the land of Persia. Even though she was orphaned and cared for by her older cousin Mordecai, she was chosen to be queen through a very vain beauty pageant. Mordecai counseled her not to reveal her Jewish heritage as she took the throne. God used Esther's beauty and poise to win the king's favor and positioned her in a pivotal point in history. God used all of who she was, even her looks, for the greater good.

This king was easily persuaded and had agreed to kill all the Jewish people throughout his kingdom. Esther could not stand for this atrocity and decided to make a request to spare their lives. Just before Esther approached the king to ask him to save the Jews, she said to her cousin, "Go and gather together all the Jews of Susa and fast for me. Do not eat or drink for three days, night or day. My maids and I will do the same. And then, though it is against the law, I will go in to see the king. If I must die, I must die" (Est. 4:16 NLT).

If I die, I die has become the theme of my life (sometimes with a little nervous giggle under my breath) as I have tried to face my own fears and build the muscle of courage in a world where it seems many have more power than me. If we look at the story of Queen Esther, we are reminded that God *will* finish what He starts. Esther knew this. Confident and courageous, she was willing to risk everything to do what God asked of her. Esther knew something we all must learn: her life was not her own.

Beth Moore, a mentor to many through her in-depth Bible studies, recounted in her Esther study the various things we fear as women: *What if ... I die, he dies, my children die, I get cancer, we lose our money, he leaves me, I get divorced ...*[1] The list goes on and on with endless possibilities. Fill in the blank for your circumstances. My fear *this week* is, What if I do not get it all done? What if I do not complete what God started in me? There is too much to do and so little time. As a busy mom, I fear I will not impart to my daughters what I was called to impart and the time will pass too quickly. I fear I will miss it. Maybe I have a little FOMO (fear of missing out). Can you relate? I fear that I will die suddenly and will have left too soon. My logical brain knows and believes God's Word in Philippians 1:6: "Being confident of this, that he who began a good work in you will carry it on to completion until the day of Christ Jesus." But my emotional brain thinks about my hairdresser who died tragically in a car accident on her way to Disneyland, my child's school friend who lost her mom to brain cancer, and the many husbands who are leaving their families because of addictions to pornography. The mind can go to endless possibilities and anxieties. The delayed text from my husband ... did he die in a car accident? Letting my child go to a birthday party ... will there be any child molesters there? Taking my child to school today ... will she be bullied? Let's be honest—we all do this to some extent.

If you struggle with fear as I do, here are a few simple truths to remember. Living in a *constant* state of fear feels like a real waste of time and energy. In the long term, fear is not good for the body or the mind, but in short bursts it can be a helpful tool to keep us alert and prayerful.[2] In fact, God created fear, since He is the one who designed our entire beings, as a purposeful warning system. However, there are also many false alarms that go off in our bodies, especially in those who have unresolved trauma in their past. This is part of PTSD (posttraumatic stress disorder), where the brain stays in fight, flight, or freeze mode even in places of safety. This brain disorder is real, and treatment is available for it. (Many of my clients have seen incredible relief from their fear as their brains and bodies heal from their past.) Instead of allowing fear to isolate us, drive us to fight mode, or cause us to shut down, we can use fear to draw closer to the Lord to find care and comfort in Him. Psalm 23 says, "The LORD is my shepherd, I lack nothing.... He guides me along the right paths for his name's sake. Even though I walk through the darkest valley, I will fear no evil, for you are with me" (vv. 1, 3–4). The presence of fear is not the culprit, but believing its lies gives it power. Stay rooted in God's Word, which says that "perfect love casts out fear" (1 John 4:18 ESV).

Our job, as moms, is not to shelter our girls but to model and teach them how to trust God throughout their lives. A mentor in my life once told me there is not one prayer for protection throughout the book of Acts but rather prayers for boldness and courage. I was blown away by this idea and started praying for boldness and courage for my own girls. Both my girls have been known to stand up for kids at recess who are being teased and to share their faith in their public school with confidence. Teaching our girls to be sensitive to the Lord's leading and to trust Him with the consequences may require us moms to do the same. Knowing there is a greater purpose to our lives gives meaning to the courageous things we get to do in this life.

What do you fear these days? How are you leaning in to God with all your might? I know that writing this book is one of the ways I am stepping out in to faith instead of feeding my fears. I am not always certain whether writing this book is for you or for me, but I am certain that it is the step I am meant to take in my own walk with God. It has taken years to get to this place in my own journey, and you are experiencing the fruit of something I never imagined would actually happen. But this book is a response to what has been birthed through living in Christ, and His perfect love is casting out all my fear.

SHE IS RESILIENT

The prophet Jeremiah drew a powerful comparison between those who trust in the Lord and those who trust in their own strength. He said,

> This is what the LORD says:
>
> "Cursed is the one who trusts in man,
>   who draws strength from mere flesh
>   and whose heart turns away from the LORD.
> That person will be like a bush in the wastelands;
>   they will not see prosperity when it comes.
> They will dwell in the parched places of the desert,
>   in a salt land where no one lives.
>
> But blessed is the one who trusts in the LORD,
>   whose confidence is in him.
> They will be like a tree planted by the water
>   that sends out its roots by the stream.
> It does not fear when heat comes;
>   its leaves are always green.
> It has no worries in a year of drought
>   and never fails to bear fruit." (Jer. 17:5–8)

Fear is a normal emotion in the human experience, yet the Word tells us that when we are like a tree whose roots are deeply grounded in a stream, we do not have to fear hard times, troubles, or persecution. In fact, fruit will come forth from the life of one who trusts the Lord. Conversely, when we put our trust in ourselves, turning away from the Lord and drawing from our own strength, we are like a parched bush in a wasteland. When life brings drought and heat, our resilience can truly be determined by where we, as moms, place our trust and how we teach our girls to draw their strength. Preparing our daughters for the path—and not preparing the path for our daughters—is the most important principle we can learn.

In recent years *resilience* has become a trendy word but for good reason. It is built only through time and hardship. In the age of next-day delivery and binge-watching, it seems that long-suffering and patience are hard to develop. Resilience is the ability to persevere and adjust when things go awry. Research shows that most people think they are resilient but are more at risk for giving up and feeling helpless than they realize. We are not born with resilience, but it is something we learn and develop. Resilient people understand that risk and failure are a part of the road to success. These people do not move away from challenges but understand how growth occurs as they face obstacles intentionally. Resilient people have anxieties and fears, but they have learned ways to cope with these emotions and have communities in place that help them find relief. The number one factor in developing resilience is the way we make meaning of our world and interpret things that happen to us outside of our control.[3] The difference between having power and feeling powerless can be as simple as the way we think.

Walking with some of the most resilient women and girls I know, I have learned a profound principle about God: He has made His people capable of moving through anything! Rebuilding, restoring, and renewing what we once thought was lost is God's primary business and is the work to which He calls His people. While not all things will be *fully* restored in this life, He is surely accomplishing a mighty work in the world, despite the way it might look to us as humans. One of our primary goals of raising girls must be to help them move through whatever difficulties life brings their way by teaching them to consider God and His ways in the midst of all of life's mess.

If we are quick to diminish hardship with typical and trite sayings, our daughters are at risk of becoming naive and vulnerable to the wolves of this world. Instead, let's equip them with the truth that empowers them to navigate life's trials. When we teach them that God uses all things for the good of His children (see Rom. 8:28), that doesn't mean we will always understand why certain things occur. We like to believe that if we do and say the right things in the right order, then all will be okay. But the reality is we cannot control most of what happens in this life. Believing otherwise is just a way to have a false sense of control or comfort ourselves, but it leaves us with a hangover that deflates our souls. There is one thing we must hold on to: no matter the why behind what happens to us, we have choices about how we respond to our circumstances. Teaching our girls the power of choice in the face of adversity can be one of the greatest gifts we ever give them.

SHE TRUSTS WHEN LIFE DERAILS

Life is unpredictable. Sometimes it takes us through twists and turns we feel unprepared to face: we receive a diagnosis; a child struggles in a way never expected; our spouse betrays us. Grief weaves a wide range of responses, including sadness, anger, bargaining, and acceptance. Grief derails us, and the path of healing from the hardships of life is a continuous process that never runs in a straight line.

Jay and Katherine Wolf recently shared their journey of a drastic life derailment and how a paradigm shift saved their lives. Married for three years, Katherine was working as a model while Jay was in law school. The big dreams of this young couple were coming true, including a shared love for their sweet six-month-old son. Life seemed to be going just as they had hoped and planned until one day when Jay found his wife slumped on the couch of their home.

She was taken to UCLA Medical Center; they had no idea what lay ahead. That day Katherine nearly died. Doctors warned Jay that, after a massive brain stem stroke at the age of twenty-six, her chances of surviving were slim. By a miracle Katherine did survive. After two months she came out of her coma.

As I sat in the audience of a crowded auditorium, listening to her harrowing story, I could hear a deep peace beneath Katherine's words. She shared that once she awoke, she could tell that time had passed by the size of her sweet baby's thighs. They were much bigger now. She tried to reach out to hold her young child, but her brain did not communicate properly with her arms. She was partially paralyzed. She could no longer hold her child, and devastation ached in every part of her body. My own maternal heart ached for her as I listened.

Now, ten years later, the Wolfs shared their story in their book *Hope Heals*. Now their testimony holds deeper meaning, presence, and identity, beyond what they could have ever imagined prior to the stroke. Katherine still lives with many disabilities and has had to fight to regain basic functions, but their story is a must-read for anyone struggling to see beyond loss. Theirs is a story that presents an alternative to unexpected derailment: hopeful transformation. When they thought they had lost everything, the Wolfs said they actually found what they were missing all along.

In their book Katherine and Jay shared their redemptive story in the most authentic way. It is not just a story of a couple who managed to find the silver lining in crisis. In other words, it is more than an attempt to bring shallow, short-lived hope to dark places. Instead, it is an honest story about how deep, abiding restoration happens outside the lines of what we might initially imagine life looking like.

I recently met Jay and Katherine. Standing in their presence, I could see their confidence was in the Lord. Katherine, a Courageous Mama, is an example of a woman who would neither give up nor become bitter.

In the depths of her greatest fear—never being the kind of mom she had wanted to be—she heard God remind her of the truths she had memorized as a young girl. At one point she questioned if God had made a mistake in keeping her alive. In that moment, she said,

I feel a deep awakening of the Word of God, which I had known since I was a little girl. I could almost hear this rapid-fire succession of the truths of Scripture, like a dispatch from God Himself.

Katherine, you are not a mistake. I DON'T MAKE MISTAKES. I know better than you know. I am God, and you're not. Remember that you were fearfully and wonderfully made in your mother's womb, and that is when the AVM formed in your brain.

There is purpose in all of this. Just wait. You'll see. There is no replacing you!...

Trust Me. I am working out EVERYTHING for your good. Don't doubt this truth just because you are in darkness now. What's true in the light is true in the dark.

I know you can't fight this. That doesn't matter. All you have to do is be still and let Me fight for you. I will complete the good work I began when I gave you new life. I will carry it on to completion. Believe that. My nature is to redeem and restore and strengthen. This terrible season will come to an end. You will suffer for a little while, and then I will carry you out of this.

You will see My goodness in the land of the living. Lean into this hope. Let it teach you how special you are. Most people will never go through this kind of hell on earth. I have chosen you. Live a life worthy of this special calling you have received.[4]

Katherine's childhood was filled with learning the Word and building a relationship with the God of the universe so that in her moment of doubt He could download the truths of His heart into hers. If you are not familiar with the Bible, those words are a string of Scriptures. Integrating God's Word into the Courageous Girls curriculum embeds God's truth in our daughters' hearts for moments when they desperately need reminding of His love and plan. I pray not only that our Courageous Girls would know the depths of God's Word for whatever roads they go down in life but also that their relationship with Him would be so secure that doubt only pushes them deeper into His presence.

Resilience and courage are not about being strong but about leaning in to the One who is stronger than anything we could ever face. I have to remind my mama heart of this daily as I send my girls into the world. I actually had my oldest daughter read *Hope Heals* as a means of dialoging with her about life's hardships and God's redemptive work. Healing does not always look the way we want, but God does far more in it than we can imagine.

The theology of suffering is a topic that moms do not want to consider much, let alone discuss with our daughters. Yet we *are* teaching our daughters daily what we think about suffering when we respond to their wounds—whether smaller wounds from the strict teacher at school or the mean volleyball coach on the court or bigger wounds from a recent divorce or racist comments at recess. The truth is, God never promised us a good life free of troubles or trials. Instead, God said He would give us abundant life (see John 10:10). Katherine is the kind of resilient woman I want to be and model to my girls. She reminds me that hope is a state of mind, not a destination. She did not arrive at hope overnight, but in the process of shifting into a hope-centered mind-set, she found the diamonds in her story that now shine brightly in a dark world.

The meltdowns about a missed parking spot or a bad-hair day have got to stop in my own life. How about in yours? Life tends not to go our way, and the practice of breathing deeply, talking to Jesus, and letting go of the belief that everyone else has it easier than us will strengthen us.

In years of ministry and counseling various populations, I have heard stories from every type of woman. Just when I think, *This woman has got it together*, I hear a little insecure girl tucked inside her that no one else can see. When we think that someone has it all or has not experienced suffering, we have been fooled by social media and the masks we try to wear. This woman does not exist, and owning this truth frees us to have compassion for ourselves and others. Moms, we need to teach our girls the stories of the Bible when God did *not* answer prayer with an immediate yes. Hebrews 11 is full of men and women of faith who never saw the ways in which God answered their deepest longings. Each of them had faith that God was working and would fulfill His promise, but it was generations before God completed what He started: "Faith is confidence in what we hope for and assurance about what we do not see. This is what the ancients were commended for. By faith we understand that the universe was formed at God's command, so that what is seen was not made out of what was visible" (vv. 1–2).

God does not always let us know what He is doing; that is why our journey is one of faith. I often wonder how I help my girls' faith grow in the everyday moments of life. Do they just believe that their laundry will get done and then *poof*—it magically appears all neatly folded in their closets? How are they learning resilience and growing their faith muscles as nine- and eleven-year-olds? The only way I am able to answer that question is by evaluating the ways in which I let them struggle. And believe me, my Merchant mama heart does not like to see my babies struggle.

This attitude reminds me of a story. There once was a man who watched a butterfly struggling to emerge from a cocoon. After hours of the butterfly's exhausted effort, the man felt concern for the butterfly. In an attempt to help release it, he took scissors to the cocoon to launch the butterfly into nature. However, after he opened the cocoon, he realized that the butterfly had wrinkled and crumbled wings and could not fly. The man had failed to understand that the butterfly's struggle was necessary for it to develop stronger wings so that it could fly. In trying to help the butterfly, the man actually limited its abilities. As moms, we need to remember that we cannot cut our child's cocoon out of our compassion or heartbreak.

We have seen the result of this type of parenting in the Millennials (born 1981–1996), generally parented by baby boomers who did not want to see their children do without any material wants. Many Millennials grew up in dual-income homes where both parents were busy working overtime. This left the average parents too exhausted to attend to their children's typical emotional needs and led to shortcut parenting. Instead of being taught the art of delayed gratification and emotional regulation, Millennials were given what they wanted and handed smartphones as little children to avoid meltdowns. This has only become worse as Millennials become parents.[5]

We need to recover the resilience factor. We can help our daughters learn how to move through difficulties rather than around them. My parents gave me the gift of not rescuing me. I remember my sixth-grade state report. I had grand plans for my visual aid about the great state of Texas, my parents' home state. I procrastinated but was left with a choice: accept my project as unfinished or slowly and steadily finish what I started. My dad helped me understand the choice, and my mom stayed by my side through my decision. I chose to finish what I started, and my mom stayed up with me to help color in all the details I had so proudly drawn on my map. As the minutes ticked away and my tears flowed, her steady presence helped me persevere.

Every time I had a difficult situation in my home, my mom or dad would discuss my options with me and give me choices to make. Every difficulty provided a crossroads. This empowered me to think through the outcomes and see the benefits of moving through rather than around. I am grateful for their foresight. They were preparing me for the road and not the road for me. I am so grateful for their deep wisdom in this area of my life. It has created an inner strength and ability to assess my choices no matter what has come my way.

Courageous Mama, consider the ways in which you are practicing delayed gratification yourself, allowing your daughter to move through difficulties with hope. Resist the temptation to rescue her, and teach her how to reframe her frustrations as a means of growing muscles to fly. As you do so, do not leave her alone to figure it all out herself. Like my mom, who sat up with me late into the night, we need to walk with our girls through the struggle. There is a time to protect our children, like when they want to run into the street or jump off a propane tank, but we need to draw a line so as not to enable our children in order to appease our own fears. We have become scared of our girls and their momentary outbursts of emotions. They desperately need us to lead the way in our own lives. Choose what you will do with your circumstances. If it's helpful, lean in to your husbands, who more often tend to avoid enabling and find it easier than us to encourage risk-taking. Take back your life from living in fear and allow God to use your story for His greater glory. He can. He will. He does.

Our daughters need to be equipped for an unkind world that will try to kill, steal, and destroy anything good in them. When we tell them the Disney message to "follow their heart, and their dreams will come true," we withhold from them the full truth and ignore the responsibility to help them deal with disappointment and heartache. The "American Idol syndrome," or fast-track-to-success prosperity gospel, has invaded our churches and our parenting. We need to reassess whether this is really the gospel message.

The Word says, "Take delight in the LORD, and he will give you the desires of your heart" (Ps. 37:4). Whether He changes our hearts to be aligned with His purposes or He puts desires in our hearts that align with His purposes, the point is to delight in the Lord. Our girls will learn from us as we choose not to ignore our fears or crumble but rather face our fears in the midst of darkness. One of my most treasured passages says, "Do not fear, for I have redeemed you; I have summoned you by name; you are mine. When you pass through the waters, I will be with you; and when you pass through the rivers, they will not sweep over you. When you walk through the fire, you will not be burned; the flames will not set you ablaze. For I am the LORD your God, the Holy One of Israel, your Savior; I give Egypt for your ransom, Cush and Seba in your stead. Since you are precious and honored in my sight, and because I love you …" (Isa. 43:1–4). These verses don't say, "If you pass through the waters …" but rather say, "*When* you …" We can be courageous throughout life's storms, which are inevitable. If you need some encouragement for your soul in the midst of feeling fear, read all of Isaiah 43. Let its truths wash over you and bring hope. Pray it over your daughter and your home.

SHE KNOWS HOW TO CALM HER ANXIETIES

It is very important to remember that having anxieties and fears is *normal* and part of the human condition; emotions are not a surprise to God. That's why so many passages in Scripture speak to them. God knows us and is not disappointed when we feel anxiety. He wants us to run to Him. It's like when our daughters get scared of the dark. For years I used a night-light and reminded them that the light represented the Holy Spirit. He is present and penetrates the darkness. Meditating on Him rather than our fears is how we regulate these human responses. Christians are especially guilty of shaming these feelings as we tell one another that we should not be anxious. That is neither helpful nor biblical. God created warning systems in our bodies for clever reasons.

There is a difference between fear and anxiety. Fear is being afraid of something we know we do not like—for example, being afraid of spiders. Anxiety is the fear of the unknown. Both fear and anxiety produce chemical reactions in the body and activate the amygdala in the downstairs brain. The more trauma in our background, the faster the amygdala activates, sending our bodies into fight, flight, or freeze mode. On the other hand, the more time we spend time grieving and truly processing our stories, the more our brains know how to rest.

Some of us have biological factors that affect our anxiety levels. Hormones, our genes, the foods we eat, and what we spend our time meditating on affect the way our brains react to the world around us. In training and equipping ministry leaders, counselors, and business leaders, Jeff and I have gone as far as to say we think the digital age and the amount of violence available for viewing have changed the makeup of our brains. Today we have larger populations of PTSD than ever before, especially among Millennials, Generation Z, and the Alpha Generation. Studies have shown that people can actually get PTSD just by watching a traumatic moment if they have any sense that it could happen to them.[6] This is informative as we consider what our girls are exposed to through their digital devices as their brains develop. Watching the news first thing in the morning might not be the best thing for our own fears and anxiety. Reading a scary book or watching a scary movie right before bed might not be the best habit either. The habits we form around our daily routines affect how quickly we can calm ourselves. Digital devices have been clinically proven to increase anxiety and stress in our bodies. Paying attention to the ways in which we spend our time will help our girls do the same. Consider how often you are using your phone, the amount of social media you are consuming a day, and the amount of tragic news entering your home through the TV and Alexa. Looking at your biology, history, habits, and daily routines will help you effectively assess factors that can be adjusted to reduce anxiety and fear.

For others, learning to reframe fear and anxiety as friends rather than foes may be the way to peace. Fear and anxiety can help us assess the outside dangers in our lives and give us permission to set healthy boundaries. For example, ignoring fear as one walks down a dark alley at night is not a good idea. We want to teach our girls to listen to these emotions and then share them with their moms, dads, and God. Ignoring emotions can lead us into years of poor decisions. I call my healthy anxiety my "red flags." I have become accustomed to listening to my body; when I feel caution in my gut, I pause long enough to pray, seek counsel, and wait until I receive further clarity. Teaching our girls to do the same will help them navigate their emotions well, producing healthier choices over time. Burnout and physical breakdown are classic examples of how ignoring our anxieties for extended periods can cause greater damage to our human systems.

Normalizing fear and anxiety is a huge factor in helping our daughters become resilient, rather than avoidant or naive. This actually creates courage because we stop having anxiety about anxiety. Seriously! Fear of our own and others' emotions can be half the battle. There is no feeling through which we cannot move. That is true both clinically and biblically. Coming up with ways we can calm ourselves is an important tool to pass on to our girls before they leave our homes. Practice is the key. In the Courageous Girls curriculum, we spend years processing this concept in tangible ways. My own five regulators are (1) talking with others because I am a verbal processor; (2) journaling my concerns and reading Scripture for truth; (3) walking in nature as I engage all five of my senses—sight, smell, hearing, taste, and touch; (4) exercising, as it provides many feel-good endorphins and releases stress; and (5) listening to music. Most girls do not know what to do in the midst of their fear and anxieties. We need five ideas at the tip of our fingers just in case one or two do not work! Sometimes we may need to do all five. Equipping our daughters with five—one for each finger on a hand—can make the difference between an impulsive decision and seeking the help they need.

As we help our daughters navigate their emotions, it's important to remember the value of validating their emotions. The ACT model from the Play Therapy Parent Coaching model[7] suggests that validating our children's emotions, keeping good boundaries, and offering our children choices is a direct way to build resilience and self-regulation skills. We can start this at any age and continue through the teen years. *A* stands for "acknowledging the emotion," *C* is for "communicating the limit," and *T* is for "targeting the alternative." An example could be what I do when I find my free-spirited daughter running around barefoot in bee-infested land. She is feeling angst in her body and needs to run. I might say, "I know you have a lot of pent-up energy and need to run free. It feels good to be barefoot in the grass [A]. However, the bees might sting your feet, so you need to wear shoes outside while you run [C]. You can get your shoes now and continue running around, or you can run around barefoot inside. You choose [T]." This simple three-step process can keep us from controlling our children by helping us honor our girls' needs and emotions while also coaching them on how to make wise decisions. Affirming our children's God-given desires to explore and try new things—or be more cautious and discerning—is part of intentional parenting. When we set limits, they feel cared for, and when we provide alternatives, they feel powerful. God is good to do the same for us in His parenting.

Feeding our faith, building resilience, and learning how to calm our anxieties and fears are vital elements in the life of a Courageous Girl. Our daughters need to know that they can move through *anything* and that we will walk with them through the fire in their younger days. We do not rescue them but give them space to build the muscles so that they learn to fly.

Takeaway

Make a list of your top five fears. Next to each fear, write a truth statement from Scripture or what you know to be true about yourself. Pray and ask God to give you opportunities to step out and practice faith. Then give God the credit when you see how He worked in and through you. Most of the time, if we look back, we can be in awe of where we are today and how we have overcome. By God's grace you are parenting a girl (or several girls) who is looking to you to teach her how to feed her faith, not her fears.

Read the book of Acts with other Courageous Mamas or with your daughter. Anytime you read the word *boldness, courage,* or *power,* study the context. Discuss the sort of danger the disciples were facing. Consider what fears you would feel if you were in their shoes. Notice what they prayed for and how God answered their prayers. This will give you and your girls more biblical accounts to remember when your own fears arise.

Take It a Step Further

Write five ways you can calm your fear and anxiety. Fear and anxiety produce physical shifts in our bodies, so make sure at least one or two options engage your body or senses with physical activities like cooking, knitting, or walking. Finally, write out five things you believe God is doing or will do in and through you. Feed your faith in a God who is able to do immeasurably more than we can ask or imagine (see Eph. 3:20). Practice the ACT model with your daughter. When she finds herself in a difficult situation, acknowledge her emotions, communicate the limits, and target an alternative. Rather than reacting, watch her grow and develop the ability to set her own limits and make choices that align with what she needs. Over time she will lean toward you rather than becoming compliant or rebellious. You've got this, Mom—God is with you.

8

She Is His Beloved

I am my beloved's and my beloved is mine.
Song of Songs 6:3

A Courageous Girl values her sexuality, a God-given and beautiful aspect of His design. The curriculum on the Courageous Girls website is a proactive way we can help shape our daughters and their view of themselves in a world that tells them they are nothing more than a body to sell for someone else's pleasure. So many moms are fearful to talk too early to their daughters about this subject for fear they will awaken something inside their innocent little girls. Other moms operate from naivete or ignorance because they have not given attention to developing their own healthy frameworks for God's good design for sex. If we are confused about what is true, healthy, and normal sexuality, our confusion will interfere with our ability to parent well.

There is no shame in acknowledging we need help in this area. The enemy has worked really hard over generations to use sexuality as a means to kill, steal, and destroy. Please do not avoid reading this chapter, as it's written with grace and a deeper understanding of the many abusive and harmful ways we ourselves have been victims and perpetuators of unhealthy sexuality. It might help you to read through this entire chapter first and then reread it to see which area God highlights to you. This topic may not be easy to approach, and your body might get triggered, but there is grace for all of us as we face our paradigms of sexuality and help our daughters do the same.

SHE THINKS CRITICALLY ABOUT CULTURAL NORMS

Our understanding of sexuality is shaped by a combination of our biology, our experiences, our education, and the unspoken rules of the culture in which we live. *Culture* is a broad term that can apply to a number of environments in which we find ourselves; our family, school, house of worship, city, country, as well as our ethnic and racial backgrounds all have cultural norms. Regardless of our stories, we all adopt the messages our communities pass on (inadvertently or purposefully) to us. Pause to consider what you learned about sexuality in childhood and adolescent years. Your adulthood was likely a response to those lessons, but you may have had some additional trauma or healthy experiences that shape your views today. Many believe sex is either a gift, a god, or gross. Which word resonates with you the most? This may help you identify the voices of your sexual time line.[1]

Sex and gender identity are at the core of many issues we face today as women and girls. The issue is so intertwined with our souls, yet the courage it takes to discuss sexuality with our children keeps most parents from ever broaching the subject. In this chapter I will share what I have learned listening to individuals and couples processing sexual betrayal, addiction, or childhood abuse. Those in my groups and in my office are teens, singles, married couples, people of faith, people not of faith, and everyone in between. These issues are quite complex, so please understand that I am not oversimplifying but rather asking moms to slow down and evaluate our concerns against the truth of God's Word and His plan for our lives.

I have never met a woman who has not been affected by the cultural sexual shift that has recently taken place. This shift toward "rape culture" has created an environment where girls no longer recognize subtle and devaluing messages about our sexuality. *Rape culture* is such a harsh phrase, but both sacred and secular experts have named this condition as they analyze music, media, social structures, universities, and workplaces of our times.[2] The recent outpouring of women stating "Me too" on social media should be enough to show that it is time to stand up against the shift toward violence against and sexualization of women in every aspect of our culture.

Healthy sexuality, from a clinical and biblical worldview, produces healthy brains, healthy relationships, and healthy family systems. *Girls & Sex* by well-respected journalist Peggy Orenstein is one of the most validating books I have read on this subject. Orenstein had no agenda but to explore the impact of current culture and how it shapes the way girls view and live out their sexuality. She explored the impact of pornography and social media, pointing out how the "selfie generation" has transformed talking about oneself as an individual developing from within to a "brand" that should be marketed, bought, and consumed.[3] Women at large are feeling the slow shift that has redefined what it means to be a woman and what it means to be sexually healthy. It's not just our daughters who are confused by these cultural shifts. How can we help our daughters when we are buying into the lies as well?

Orenstein interviewed over seventy girls and then bravely revealed the realities girls are facing today. She spoke with them about their self-identified sexual identities. Many of the girls interviewed had done internet searches on whether they were transgender, gay, or bisexual based on a dislike for "girl" norms like dance classes, wearing makeup, or wearing feminine clothing. Relying on Google for answers to questions of sexual identity can become life altering. Orenstein responded with this profound statement: "When we've defined femininity for their generation so narrowly, in such a sexualized, commercialized, heteroeroticized way, where is the space, the vision, the celebration of other ways to be a girl?"[4] Though Orenstein and I might take different stances on why girls struggle and how they might make sense of their identify formation, we agree that being a girl is defined too narrowly.

My dad originally wanted boys (but eventually saw the delight of raising daughters), so as a child, I found myself identifying more with activities that men enjoyed. I was quite capable of keeping up with my male peers. I outbenched the football players during my freshman bodybuilding class. I could not wait to run home and brag to my dad (who still tells the story today). I did not want to be a part of girl drama. I did not wear much makeup, and I avoided painting my nails to avoid being too girlie. I was a tomboy for years and preferred a more natural look. If I had grown up with the messaging of today and had the internet to do a search, I might have questioned my gender identity. I cannot know for sure, but I do know that because I grew up prior to the gender revolution we find ourselves in today, the idea was never planted in my mind. The cultural norm in my world was that being a girl was broad enough so that I could be both strong *and* a girl. Despite the attempts to the contrary, the expanding definitions of our day actually seem to be narrowing our gender perspectives. We are too quick to define our children and let them discern their own sexuality and gender identity. From a neuroscientific and human developmental point of view, a third grader is not ready to make those kinds of decisions, though it is becoming a more common and accepted norm. We would not let her or encourage her to choose a mate or a career or drive before she's ready, so why would we encourage her to decide if she is male or female?

God ordains each person with purpose. In that purpose, He provides a lot of freedom with a few boundaries. I happily identify as a woman. In my twenties I wrestled with what it means to be feminine. I have since embraced wearing makeup, accessorizing, and shopping—all stereotypically feminine things. But I'm still a business owner, coach, consultant, and teacher of men and women. I like being strong. I'm not sure I can outbench any men today, but I do help my husband lift and move heavy objects on our property regularly. Being physically strong has come in handy! My husband might miss the more natural woman he fell in love with, since our household budget has absorbed some of the habits I have picked up over the years, but I'm proud that I can still throw a football and gut my own fish.

When we try to construct an identity for ourselves, we will ultimately feel unsatisfied. The thirst in our souls will remain. We are confused people, on all issues, and this is why we need direction from our Creator. Please hear my heart; my views are not based on theoretical circumstances. I have sat and considered the issues of sexuality in the most personal ways, from the effects of sexual abuse, sexual betrayal, gender identity, premarital sex, sex trafficking, and more. I have walked with real people and have chosen to join them where they are, in the center of their pain, with compassion. In the written form, these topics can sound trite and merely cognitive. But I have tied my very being to these words. For most of my forty years, I have been faced with these issues in my family of origin, friendships, community, ministry, and professional counseling experience. I am not claiming to be an expert on this topic, but I might know a little more than the average mama.

Fa*Courageous*

SHE VALUES BOTH MALE AND FEMALE CONTRIBUTIONS

Questioning our sexuality is ultimately about finding our identity and purpose. "Who I am meant to be?" is a complex question and must be explored over time, in relationship, and with careful consideration of the Word. A teenage girl who is not sexually aroused by her boyfriend pressuring her to explore his body should not wonder if she's a lesbian. Similarly, a woman who is often disgusted by her sexual relationship with her husband—who is addicted to porn and exhibits no emotional intimacy—need not question her identity. The young girl who is excited that her female friend might have a crush on her, particularly if this relationship is the only place where she has found love, attention, and human connection, does not have cause to question her sexual orientation. In all these areas, coaching is needed more than an exploration of sexual orientation.

Our sexuality is partly influenced by our biology and mostly shaped by life experiences and cultural influences. When I was a girl, I would hold hands with my best girlfriends. It felt safer to dance with them at the eighth-grade dance than with the boys. (Let's be honest, the boys were quite stinky and awkward.) Girlfriends are better in so many ways when we are growing up, at least until boys move beyond their hormonal shifts and start to mature. It's no secret that we are feeling "the great demise of guys"[5] because of "the digital invasion."[6] Boys lack social skills more than ever, and our girls are desperate for someone to look them in the eye. Guiding our girls through all the experiences, questions, exposure, and inward processing is a powerful, needed, and sacred gift of being a mom.

Gender matters. Though this book is about girls, we must include a little information about boys when exploring these subjects. The Bible is not the only literature that says gender matters. In the age of gender fluidity, it's important to speak to the glaring biological evidence that science still supports key differences between males and females. Our predetermined chromosomes and genitalia are not the only defining factors, though the current popular thought might claim differently. Psychologist and physician Leonard Sax, MD, PhD, wrote, "The failure to recognize and respect sex differences in child development has done substantial harm.... The lack of awareness of gender differences has had the unintended result of reinforcing gender stereotypes. The result is more girls uploading sexualized and provocative photos to their Instagram and Snapchat and more boys spending hours playing violent video games in which they pretend to be macho warriors and villains.... Just as important, the growing confusion about gender is contributing to a rise in anxiety and depression among girls and disengagement among boys."[7]

Though boys are part of God's amazing design, our boys are struggling on a greater systemic plane. Raising boys who not only value women but also see their God-given design is a huge calling and may be addressed at some point in another book.

If we consider the ways in which males and females are created from birth, we can better understand their day-to-day interactions at home, school, and work. Hearing and smelling senses are more acute in females, making a middle school girl more likely to hear a teacher's instructions and be turned off by a boy's body odor, and making a mother more sensitive to the voices of her children calling when she is trying to have a romantic moment with her spouse. These biological factors affect many aspects of how we relate to our world. When a husband does not hear his wife's words the first time, could it be because his hearing does not pick up the same frequencies as a woman's? When a son has a hard time settling down after a long day at school, could it be because he just needs a change of environment, where he can exert physical energy, compete, and take risks?

Considering the science on gender can help us be attuned to better solutions for our relational mishaps.

According to Jonathan Haidt, a social psychologist at New York University Stern School of Business, and Lenore Skenazy, the greater problem for our society is that we have become an overprotective society where children have been "protected" from exploring (for example, climbing trees) because they could be easily hurt. Due to the overarching pendulum swing from latchkey kids to overly supervised and highly scheduled kids, children are not learning the basic skills to move into adulthood, and the implications are just now coming to the forefront.[8] Boys are not learning (as they would have in former generations) how to use their natural bent toward independence and adventure to take risks for their families when they become adults. Avoiding harm and playing it safe has become the norm.

"The demise of guys" refers to the idea that fewer men are going to college, committing to marriage, and leaving Mom and Dad's couch to earn a living. This reality is partly due to addictions to pornography and oversexualization in our culture. But it also may be due to devaluing what maleness innately brings to furthering our human race and how it reflects God's character. Women's response to years of oppression has been to turn the tide and make men feel inferior. You may not agree, but look around. You will easily find women saving men in movies, making fun of men on sitcoms, and reducing men with the casual side comment "They want only one thing." When we devalue men, we contribute to their demise.

Let's pause and consider why this matters in raising our daughters to be courageous. How we view men, talk about men, raise our boys, and treat our husbands helps our daughters choose to value men and boys as well. Our words, actions, and subtle responses can lead our girls to see males as part of God's plan, not people to be feared, ignored, or dismissed. When Courageous Girls learn about God's value and

purpose for men and how He values them, they will be able to identify the counterfeits. They will neither seek men for their identity and
worth nor treat men with disrespect or disregard. It's all integrated
in this greater systemic shift we long to see. We have come so far in
valuing women over the years, but the pendulum swing might have
gone too far. It is important to consider our own biases, stories, and
cultural norms related to gender roles, stay educated on the current
data, and funnel everything through the lens of Scripture as we teach
our daughters to live out of whom God designed them to be.

SHE IS EDUCATED ON THE RELEVANT ISSUES

In an age when we are moving from a binary culture (male and
female) to a pluralistic culture (with a growing number of gender
types and sexual orientations since each person can define his or her
own descriptor), we cannot lose sight of the science of gender. Be
educated moms. Gender statistics have not really changed, though
our interpretation of the evidence may be changing. God created
male and female as a beautiful reflection of the triune God (see
Gen. 1:27). I believe the design of male and female is a beautiful
thing. The collaboration of the two genders can breed a powerful
challenge, rounding out our humanity and causing us to think and
live outside our own nature. Moving beyond ourselves is a growing
opportunity for all of us and takes daily practice. For a single mom,
hanging out with other couples and having male friends can be powerful ways to model to your girls that not all men are unsafe, unkind,
and "after only one thing." One gender without the other can feel
lopsided because it reflects only part of our triune God's nature.

The evidence of gender research reveals that most girls are more
relationally aware than boys and have more complex responses to
their environments. They have brains that are more integrated and

allow more access between the emotional and logical parts of the brain. Because of the brain development of men, most are focused on one thing at a time and therefore can compartmentalize more easily. Both of these tendencies have purpose and work beautifully in tandem. Letting go of our identities as male and female can become a slow departure from the truth of science and, in a way, like the clay pot telling the potter that he made a mistake. Becoming educated on our children's, spouses', and colleagues' gender differences can open our eyes to the wonder of how we can partner together.

I have helped people in their search for healthy sexuality for twenty years. At the core of both men and women is a longing to be known, loved, significant, and accepted. We keep trying to meet our legitimate needs in illegitimate ways. Seeking only the orgasm, the romantic experience, or the high-intensity dopamine fix has created social epidemics and cultural addictions. This mind-set has infused our daily habits, whether we like it or not. We have to stand up and lead our girls. It is not good leadership to leave them to discern their own sexuality, decide how they present their bodies to the world, or experiment in order to discover their identity and purpose in life.

The Hawaiian-themed Disney movie *Moana* has an amazing scene at the end. Moana is called to restore the heart to a lava monster, Te Ka, which had been stolen long ago by the demigod Maui. As many Disney princesses do, Moana sings to Te Ka and bravely faces her fire-throwing anger. In singing, "This is not who you are. You know who you are," she successfully restores Te Ka's heart. The lava, Te Ka's primary defense, subsides, and Te Ka's true beauty is revealed.[9] It gets me every time!

This is our call: to remind our girls, our boys, ourselves, other moms, our husbands, and the world around us, "This is not who you are; you know who you are." Humans are not brands to be sold, and they are not to be used or minimized as body parts. We are not meant to give of ourselves so intimately in such shallow and casual ways. The gift of sex has been turned into a dirty tool and has lost its meaning.

Being confused and disoriented about gender identities, roles, and expressions of our sexual nature is not a new thing. It is an age-old issue for humanity, and God's ways have brought clarity time and time again. We can read story after story in the Old and New Testaments about the variety of ways God's people struggled to regulate their sexuality or even used sexuality to cause great devastation. (For example, Gen. 19; 38; Lev. 18; 20; 2 Sam. 11; 13; Rom. 1.) Sex has been reduced to gratifying lustful pleasures or performing duty. Because of this, we should not be surprised when those outside the church make sex the central issue. Paul warned the church against this practice. The church in Corinth provides a classic example of how the church integrated cultural norms into ecclesial practices, and Paul made it clear that these behaviors were unacceptable according to God's ways (see 1 Cor. 5:1–2). As we help our daughters walk through questions of gender, sexual identity, and healthy partnership between males and females, we must remember God's perspective. The human ways have drawn us astray, but when we trust in the Lord and in all our ways acknowledge Him and His ways, He will make our paths straight (see Prov. 3:5–6).

SHE ADDRESSES SEXUALITY WITHOUT SHAME

Sexual relationships were originally designed for six reasons: to create a unique bond between a husband and wife, to provide comfort, to enjoy pleasure, to create life, to reflect intimate knowing, and to express lifelong commitment.[10] Sex was designed as the expression of our love for each other. This beautiful picture calms many of our hearts as we consider the purpose behind the design. The enemy and the selfish ways of humanity have tainted its value.

There is deep and rich theology around sexually intimacy. Sadly many churches rarely teach it correctly. Women use sex to keep their husbands either satisfied or from being unfaithful. Many have full disdain for the act. Teens and girls use sexuality as a means to get love and attention. We are trying to find love in all the wrong places. These oversimplified examples are not to minimize the issues but to help us see what lies beneath the surface for most of us. Sex has become a dreaded topic for many moms, and their daughters' uncomfortable responses might indicate the conversations needed along the road of life.

> Hear, O Israel: The LORD our God, the LORD is one. You shall love the LORD your God with all your heart and with all your soul and with all your might. And these words that I command you today shall be on your heart. You shall teach them diligently to your children, and shall talk of them when you sit in your house, and when you walk by the way, and when you lie down, and when you rise. You shall bind them as a sign on your hand, and they shall be as frontlets between your eyes. You shall write them on the doorposts of your house and on your gates. (Deut. 6:4–9 ESV)

We cannot expect our girls to know or understand how to live out loving God with all our hearts, souls, and might if we do not model and address sexuality as women. This includes acknowledging our changing bodies and sexuality. If we do not lead our girls, the world will. Saying nothing about our sexuality can speak louder than our words. When we speak vaguely, we leave open holes for others to fill. There is a process of talking with our girls at appropriate developmental stages, equipping them to understand and appreciate their uniquely female bodies. In the context of safe conversations, we also need to give them a foundation by teaching them about God's profound design for sex, which passes on a passion for purity before and during marriage. (Keeping the marriage bed pure, according to Hebrews 13:4, applies to before and after the wedding.) The Courageous Girls curriculum was designed to help us tackle these difficult topics at each stage of life. Moving toward such conversations about biological changes, crushes, dating, gender identity, and pornography allows us to normalize a daughter's curiosity and help calm her nerves about these subjects, reducing her chance of falling prey to another person's agenda. Knowing biblical and clinical truths about the matter can help her have a voice, say no, and get help if she is ever in a situation where she could be violated.

Talking about sex is not just to help our daughters avoid being a victim of offenders. Sex touches something deep in our souls. We have tried to turn that lever off in order to be seen in a culture that oversexualizes, but it has not worked. Let's consider how out of balance we have become regarding sexuality, gender, and body-image issues. These statistics are always changing, and I fear that by the time this book is in print, they will be outdated and even more extreme. Middle school girls are exploring oral sex as a "safer" form of sex. The average American girl has had intercouse by the time she is seventeen, and by nineteen, three-fourths have already had sex.[11] By the time a girl graduates from college, she is likely to have experienced one form of sexual assault or sexual abuse, regardless of her background. A recent study conducted by the Harvard Graduate School of Education found that 87 percent of women aged eighteen to twenty-five reported having experienced sexual harassment in their lifetime; many report that they have never talked with their parents about how to avoid these situations.[12] Depending on the source, same say that one in three girls have been sexually abused by a trusted person in her her life (this is based on recognizing that 60 percent of abuse goes unreported). One in two girls thinks her ideal body weight is less than she actually weighs.[13] Every girl has been affected by the cultural norms of being pretty. Self-harming behaviors such as cutting, eating disorders, pornography addictions, and even suicide are at the highest rates ever in many age groups and are rising still. The average girl is first exposed to pornography between the ages of eight and eleven years old.

The reality is that the sex and pornography industries are looming over our homes, destroying our marriages, and teaching our children that we are merely animals driven by our uncontrolled visceral and primal needs. We spend billions on beauty products, gym memberships, and buttocks reconstruction—for what? So that we will be loved? So that we will be seen? So that someone will notice our beauty and fulfill our longing to be cherished?

Mamas—let's get these statistics into our heads! Tear away the veil of indifference and the comforting mantras (*That's not my daughter*) that we replay in our heads. The daughters of many good mamas have been in my counseling office telling me things she believed she could not tell you. In those moments I desperately wanted *you* to be the one to help her. That is the original design for parenting. You can be her greatest advocate and guide. She is watching you! If we do not actively participate in processing these issues at a developmentally appropriate pace, the culture will surely beat us to the punch!

SHE PLACES SEX IN ITS RIGHTFUL PLACE

Let us finish this chapter by discussing a healthy view of sexual intimacy from both a biblical and a clinical worldview. Detectives who investigate counterfeit money confess that when they study the authentic dollar bill in-depth, they are able to spot the fake one faster. This principle can be applied all over the place, especially in the realm of healthy sexuality.

Sex, in its rightful place within the context of marriage, is like eating dessert: it is meant to be the end of a nutritious meal, not the main course. Using sex as the means for any couple to sustain a lifelong connected marriage is like living on dessert. Sex is meant to add to the greater enjoyment within the relationship, not be the focus. Grandma Bowerly always said, "Eat dessert first," which has become a fun tradition our family has adopted, and my children relish it on special occasions. (In fact, I just took my youngest out for ice cream before we ventured to dinner. We both giggled as we delighted in our treats!) But we all know that even though it's exciting to eat dessert first, it can spoil our dinner and leave our bodies with unintended side effects in the long haul. If we ate this way on a regular basis, our bodies would have all kinds of negative symptoms, such as heart disease, diabetes, and low energy. Sex is intended to be enjoyed when a husband and wife have invested in the hard work of preparing and digesting emotional intimacy, commitment, and shared meaning. Otherwise experienced, such as in premarital sex or as the only means of expressing love in a marriage, sex will become detrimental to one's spiritual, emotional, and relational health.

Sex is something worth waiting for. Many of us adults express our own concerns about having sex too early in our lives or not knowing the long-term negative effects of premarital sex. Messages like "Just don't" or "If you do, use protection" offer little help. Viewing sex in movies or pornography—or learning by experience—has been the main teacher for most. Some mamas project their own painful stories onto their girls, not telling them the mistakes they made and how they would live differently if they had a second chance. While words may not be expressed, daughters can feel the shame that leaks from their mothers' unresolved past. Another approach for mamas has been the "holier than thou" attitude, making daughters feel shame for even having a desire for sexual pleasure. The truth is that God created us as sexual beings; our responsibility is to learn how to relegate our sexuality to its rightful place. Just like with our emotions, food appetites, and spending habits, regulating and making wise choices that leave us feeling whole and not harmed are the keys to health.

As I have processed sexuality at every level, the root of the issue for all people always comes down to a longing for authentic connection and emotional intimacy. Using sex as a means to escape, cope, get or keep love, find value, or define ourselves is a harmful way to relate to sex and will lead us to a dead end. Sex is meant to be the *result* of deep emotional intimacy, not the producer of it. When sex is brought into a relationship prior to marriage, in any form, there are damaging effects. Our sexuality is reinforced by whatever we have been exposed to: pornography, abuse, promiscuity, shame, spiritual legalism, and so forth. Similarly, the risk of lung cancer is much higher for one who smokes than for those who do not. Protecting and honoring our bodies and their intended sexuality are means to a healthier sexual relationship in marriage. We can talk to our girls about purity and premarital sex within this context. Here is what relationship and sexual-formation experts know:

1. Women want to be chosen. When sex is simply an act of ecstasy or orgasm and is reduced to a momentary pleasure, it produces a feeling of objectification.

2. Relationships where sexual boundaries were honored prior to marriage have higher levels of trust than in relationships where the boundaries were crossed.

3. When people can regulate their sexuality prior to marriage, which simply means they will not give in to its every craving, they are more likely candidates for faithfulness in marriage.[14]

4. Monogamy produces greater satisfaction in sex and overall relationships than any other sexual relationship.

5. When our "No, thank you" is honored in the sexual relationship, our "No, thank you" is honored in all parts of the relationship. Boundaries are crossed in all areas of a relationship when one partner is unable to hear "No" to his or her needs and wants. It's like a two-year-old who wants a cookie. If she can't hear "No" now, she won't hear it when she's a teenager.

6. Sex is one of the most intimate acts, though it has been diluted by our culture to what a wave or handshake used to mean. Nowadays one does not need to know another well to have a physical encounter. The ironic thing is that the Scripture verse "Adam *knew* his wife" uses the same Hebrew word as is used for God *knowing* us. This has huge implications for the intent of sex, the spiritual connection it can create, and the vulnerability it requires. Engaging in sex without vulnerability and emotional intimacy requires great dissociation from our hearts, minds, and bodies.

7. Sex offers us a huge dose of oxytocin (a bonding hormone) and dopamine (a feel-good hormone). Oxytocin is the same hormone produced by a nursing mom and her baby so that they form an attachment. When sex is used in casual relationships, we are messing with the neural pathways in our brains that are trying to make healthy connections. The dopamine fix is meant to keep us coming back to each other. Sexual intimacy can help us feel closer to and enjoy a precious gift with the most intimate person in our lives. I think God was pretty clever to make this the final step in our consummation of marriage. When you have committed to another person in covenant, then you bond with that person.

8. Any sexual act that is connected to our private areas, or what we would cover with our bathing suits, is considered part of the sexual experience. I might hug another man and give my father a kiss on the cheek, but as a married woman, I would not engage in any other type of physical behavior with another male. This can help us define what is unacceptable outside of marriage when a girl asks how far she can go. Behaviors like sending photos, touching body parts, long kisses, petting, and even oral sex can be justified by many but should be of concern when we teach our girls to value their bodies and their sexuality.

9. In unhealthy circles, women are told they should not withhold sex from their husbands because sex is the way husbands feel loved. The truth is that men must learn how to love outside of sex and to regulate their sexuality in order to honor their wives. First Corinthians speaks to both marriage partners. The wife does not have authority over her own body but yields it to her husband. In the same way, the husband does not have authority over his own body but yields it to his wife (see 7:4). This is a reflection of the divine dance. If both are giving, then there is safety and respect. If one seeks his or her own pleasure without consideration of the other or seeks his or her needs outside of the relationship, then he or she truly misses the essence of the design.

God's design was for men and women to give to and serve each other. In some cases, giving to your husband by making sex quick can be helpful for both partners. In other cases, saying "No, thank you, but let's try again this weekend" is a helpful approach that gives honor and respect to ourselves. The truth is, a husband will not die without sex, contrary to some popular teachings. I can promise that. It is up to a husband (or wife) to regulate his (or her) sexuality outside of masturbation, pornography, or annoying the other spouse until she (or he) says yes. Self-gratification is not the purpose of sex. Sex was created for a husband and wife to express mutual sacrifice in the context of a committed lifelong relationship and for both partners' enjoyment, exploration, and edification.

In my office or at workshops, I often hear the question "Would you buy a car before you researched it?" Depending on your wiring, you may spend months comparing consumer reports, visiting various dealers, conducting test drives, and checking the engine with a professional. Having sex before marriage is similar to signing on the dotted line and buying a car prior to doing the homework needed for the purchase. The neurobiological and theological reasons for sex are that it is meant to bond us and create life. This amazing act is meant to be the celebration *after* all the research (praying, seeking counsel, having others give feedback) and demonstrated consistent track record. Do the hard work of exploring who a person is, marry that person, and *then* enjoy the gift of sex.

In summary, waiting to have sex until after marriage helps to establish trust, self-regulation skills, and fidelity. In a broader sense, it helps partners practice how to love and solve conflict outside of sex, which demonstrates that our inherent worth extends beyond what we do for each other. Hopefully by the time we choose to marry someone, we are also ready to parent a child, which is an obvious side effect of sexual intercourse. This kind of commitment requires a larger meaning and purpose than "because the Bible tells me so." Contrary to what many hope or believe, having sex before marriage does not lead to a happy and healthy relationship. If you have crossed those lines, there is still hope. God is always ready to redeem when we are ready to align ourselves with His ways.

SHE CHOOSES AND IS CHOSEN

Knowing and exercising one's voice, as well as making God-empowered choices, are pivotal aspects of a Courageous Girl. A valuable example of this is the act of being chosen *and* choosing whom we date, whom we marry, and whom we engage sexually. While it may seem that this aligns with the cultural norm "I determine my destiny," it actually runs counter to that message. Biblical choice is rooted in a deep truth communicated again and again in God's Word: we are loved and can have intimacy with God and others outside of sex. Sex is not the means to intimacy, and the desire for intimacy takes different forms in men and women. No matter how strong they are, all girls want to be protected, pursued, and cherished. No matter how passive some might be, all men want to protect, pursue, and cherish. This may feel outdated or archaic, but from the data in my office, this has been continually proven to be true.

There is so much to say about sexuality, but for the sake of helping mamas and daughters, let's consider some practical ways we can emphasize the value of our daughters' bodies and practice what it feels like when their "No" is respected. Teaching and practicing how to honor our bodies, even in the ways we care for them practically, establishes a firm foundation for healthy sexuality and body image in the teen and adult years. This helps our daughters defend themselves against those who want to harm them both in and outside of close relationships. Initiating dialogue about these subjects with our daughters in their earliest developmental years is the best way we can help them. Here are some other practical ways we can help them value their bodies and respect their "No."

1. Did you know that research has shown that healthy tickle games with our daughters develop confidence, resilience,

intimacy, and other wonderful relationship skills? Starting from the beginning, many of us play tickle games with our girls. When they say "Stop," we stop. Then we say out loud, "I respect your 'No.' " So many in the world will not respect our "No." If we are being honored in our homes, we will learn to set clear boundaries for ourselves. Otherwise we will normalize crossing boundaries through simple games like tickling.

2. Around age three or four, we can help our daughters learn to value their special bodies by encouraging them to shut the door when they go to the bathroom. Talk about who can help them wipe, take a bath, or get dressed. Limit this to safe people, and explain that their special parts (those covered by their bathing suits) are for the bathroom and cleaning. As our daughters age, discuss other purposes for those special areas. Talk about good touch (such as wanted hugs, cuddling, holding hands) and bad touch (such as hitting, touching privates as a child, or not respecting someone's "No"). This also means not forcing your daughter (or children) to kiss Uncle John or get a hug from the teacher. Our cultural norms and the need to be polite can quickly override the greater and most needed message that people are to respect our "No." This also means that showering or taking baths with siblings, cousins, or anyone else beyond the age of two can become confusing, and it's important to consider the cost in light of the inconvenience of bathing your children separately or skipping a bath if necessary.

3. When your daughter is changing, without a shameful tone or condemning body language, remind her that her body is special and she can change in private. Changing in public spaces in the home and running around naked

(developmentally, gender awareness begins between ages two and three) can be confusing if we think about the greater vision for our girls. Remember, teaching about modesty without shame, value beyond our bodies, and using our voices to remain safe and within our God-given power and control will help your daughter build confidence in whom God designed her to be. This type of norm becomes natural as your daughter uses the restroom at school, changes in locker rooms, and goes to other people's homes. She will have her own discernment to value her special parts and learn tricks to change but recognize it's not because she needs to fear being sexualized but rather because her body is not just for anyone. This takes lots of practice, ongoing dialogue, answering real-life questions throughout all the stages of life, and continuing to do our own work regarding our sexual paradigms.

4. Modesty, an issue we address in the Courageous Girls curriculum at every developmental stage, varies from home to home. The most basic issues include talking about what we are wearing and the motive behind why we are wearing it. It is important to teach our daughters that it is not their job to keep every boy and man from lusting after them by wearing a turtleneck or swimming in their clothes. Remember, the Bible teaches men (and women) to regulate their own sexuality in a way that it does not rule them. Modesty is "having or showing a moderate or humble estimate of one's merits, importance, etc.; free from vanity, egotism, boastfulness, or great pretensions."[15] This sounds pretty biblical to me. Often today's outfits are intended to show off a physical asset we were given. The cultural message is, if you have them (breasts, tight abs, cute buttocks, long legs, etc.),

you should flaunt them. What does that mean when we do not like our bodies? In either case, using clothes to find our worth leaves us feeling empty. Our dress can be a form of expressing our creativity, meeting a practical need for comfort, or preparing for the task at hand. Showing off our private parts is not one of the main purposes and talking about this with our girls, even when they are little, can help them own their sense of discernment. By late elementary school, taking your daughter shopping and inviting her to think through these issues with you will only add to her sense of worth and enjoyment of clothes.

5. Let your girls practice letting someone open the door for them. Intentionally talk to them about how boys should treat them. We often pause TV shows, movies, and songs to talk through the messages that are being promulgated. Is that girl being valued? Is that boy treating her with respect? Recently my family watched *Back to the Future*, a movie my husband and I used to love. We completely forgot that in the movie there is a scene where the main bully tries to sexually assault a girl. There was little shown in the movie, but we paused and immediately discussed what it means when a boy is treating a girl that way. We asked whose fault it was (his, of course) and questioned what the girl could do. Left alone, our girls could have drawn a variety of conclusions. Given that sexual aggression has become so normal, our girls need to know that a man should treat her with love, kindness, and respect, and honor her "No"! If he has a pattern of not honoring her "No," he is no longer the man for her.

6. Continue to give your daughter choices in her daily routines (within reason). When she is age two, let her choose if she

wants the apple sauce or the pear. When she is five, let her choose if she wants to wear the blue shirt or the red shirt. Choices start small and they grow as our daughters grow. Making every decision for your daughter will only cause one of two things: (1) a girl who needs to be controlled and attracts controlling relationships or (2) a rebellious spirit who will go right when you suggest left. Choices come in all shapes and sizes, but working out our own pride and emotional needs through our daughters can scar them for life. As parents, we need to provide limits (as God does for us) because this models greater principles for life.

Let me end with a real-life example. My nine-year-old daughter has a sense of style and picked out a pretty cute outfit. I can trust her ability to coordinate her outfits and discern how she feels in her clothes. It was a rushed morning (I am sure you can relate), and it was time to get in the car. I told her, "Grab your shoes and hop in the car." I did not think twice until she was stepping out of the car to walk into school and I looked down to see her wearing her outdoor chicken coop boots. In my surprise I exclaimed, "You wore your boots?" She looked back at me with lowered brows and shame on her face. At that moment I knew she was embarrassed and likely confused. I was ultimately concerned about her carrying chicken poop throughout the school hallways more than I was concerned about how she looked. This was what I communicated, and she immediately responded, "I thought I was supposed to wear shoes for the after-school playdate at our friend's farm." *Hmmm, good point,* I thought. In that split second, I had a choice. I could continue to feel my own embarrassment and shame about letting my daughter deliver fertilizer all over the school or recognize the greater opportunity to let my daughter have power in her own world. (Honestly, they were not the cutest pair of shoes with her oh-so-cute outfit, so the decision was even harder.) I chose to honor her decision, by the help of the Holy Spirit, and owned my tone. It does not always go that way, but I followed up with her after school to make sure she knew that she was not in the wrong and encouraged her to think through her choice next time.

Choices are woven into every part of our lives, including parenting. They do not always directly relate to sexuality, but let me relay this as clearly as I can: the messages we learn about our power and control in our world will directly affect the kind of relationships we attract, the motives for our sexual behavior, and the ways we illegitimately use our bodies to gain what was lost.

Courageous Mama, I am for you. God is for you. And you *can* do this. Your daughter needs you, and it is never too late to start moving toward health. Lord, help us to "do all things through [Christ] who strengthens [us]" (Phil. 4:13 ESV). Amen!

Takeaway

If you have not addressed your own sexual story, recognize that may interfere with your ability to parent your daughter well. Start by creating a sexual time line[16] and naming the lessons you have learned about your sexuality and gender identity through your own life experiences. Consider asking a professional, trusted friend, or mentor to come alongside you, and start processing your own pain. You are not alone. Until we grieve, forgive, and receive the grace offered us, our past will haunt us like a person buried alive; you never know when it will come up and try to grab your leg! It's an awful depiction, but that's the point! You are courageous. Addressing your story will give you the greatest ability to help your daughter(s).

Take It a Step Further

Evaluate your daughter's age and assess the needs she might have in her developmental stage. Go to the list above and discern which practice you want to integrate this month. Look for opportunities to discuss body care, modesty, and the messages about sexuality in your community. Answer any of her questions. Normalize this type of conversation. If you are doing the Courageous Girls curriculum with a group of other moms, make sure you lean in to them for prayer and wisdom.

9

She Dreams ... Big

Jesus comes to people and invites us to be what-if? *people.
He said to his early followers, "I want you to imagine a
kingdom—the* real *magic kingdom. Imagine a kingdom
where the last are first, the least are greatest, the servants
are heroes, the weak are strong, and the marginalized are
loved and cherished. Imagine a world where outsiders
become insiders, where people who lose their lives end
up finding them, where people who die to themselves
and their guilt and their sin and their selfishness end
up being brought to life. Imagine that your little broken
story can become part of a larger story that ends well."*

John Ortberg, *All the Places to Go*

Living a life invested in the things of Jesus means we are *what-if*
people. Courageous Girls are able to be confident in God because
they have gradually learned He is in control and has a greater vision
for His people. Though we are the apple of God's eye, we are not the
center of the greatest story ever told. *He* is. When we begin to see the

world through the heart of God, we are humbled by the gift of being used in His greater plan.

SHE SEES BEYOND HERSELF

I have a list of quotes in the front of my Bible. C. S. Lewis's words are written at the top: "I believe in Christianity as I believe that the Sun has risen, not only because I see it, but because by it I see everything else."[1] Everything in life is clearer when we encounter Jesus and the light of His grace. Darkness dims when we can see by His light and even become the light in a world desperate to see hope in the flesh. John 1:5 says, "The light shines in the darkness, and the darkness has not overcome it." This light is Jesus.

Being in relationship with God, who is full of grace and mercy, reminds us that we are right where we are supposed to be. He has created us for such a time as this and will equip us with the resources needed to be attuned to those for whom His heart beats. Wherever we are in life, He still moves in and through us. Despite us, He does His thing. We may think in terms of "if only …, then …" (when I get more money, when my kids are older, or when my marriage is better). The list is endless. Yet, in God's economy, He does not need anything outside Himself to make something out of nothing. God spoke and the world was created out of empty darkness. Now that is power!

When we choose to follow Christ, that same Spirit of God is in us. We are literally in courage. God is the most courageous being and He is in us. He wants to do something in you and then through you. There is a sign in our guest bathroom that I read almost every day. It says, "If you could not fail, what would you do?" You are experiencing the fruit of that message as you read this book! I am not extraordinary. I do, however, believe in an extraordinary God who *loves* to work in and through His people. All He wants is our yes, and He clearly respects our no.

It is so easy to get caught in the here-and-now rat race of life: focusing on the laundry, the meals, the dishes, the errands, the sports, the homework, and the laundry (yes, laundry is listed twice on purpose). Before we know it, the week is over and the haze of busyness has sucked up all our energy. Can I hear an amen? In the book *Screwtape Letters*, C. S. Lewis showed that a great tactic of the enemy is to keep Christians busy.[2] It's not a creative strategy, but it's surely effective.

It takes incredible discipline to stop and listen. Listen to what our deepest invitation is from our Creator. This is what a quiet time can help us do: see beyond the ordinary of life and lift our heads to a greater destiny, one that is ordained by the King of the universe. There are seasons in life when we must embrace the daily tasks. There are other seasons when we must receive from others in order to heal, find comfort, and later offer that comfort to others. These are called seasons for a reason. None of us, even moms, are meant to focus on completing in the day-to-day tasks of life unless we know without a shadow of a doubt it is where God has asked us to be. There is no place I would rather be than in the pocket of His plan, and that can look different for each of His children. If you are a mom of several children, you can understand His delight in and encouragement of the unique strengths of each of His children.

Andy Crouch challenged "safe Christianity" when he said, "Vulnerability that leads to flourishing requires risk."[3] This is not the kind of risk we take when we choose not to wear a seat belt while driving around town. He means the kind of risk that requires us to take time out of our safe communities and engage an impoverished one or travel to where we could get ill. I'm talking about the kind of risk Jesus took by touching a leper who was considered outcast, unclean, and contagious and by spending a moment with the children despite their lack of value to adults in their culture (see Matt. 8:3; 19:13–14). It might mean a great marriage. It might mean living with simplicity. It might mean serving our communities without any expectations of getting something in return. I cannot tell you what it means for you and your daughter, but what I can tell you is that we are not to live inside a box, in safety, and expect to feel fulfilled or alive. That was not the design.

In his book *Culture Making: Recovering Our Creative Calling*, Crouch said,

> The bigger the change we hope for, the longer we must be willing to invest, work and wait for it.…
>
> I wonder what we Christians are known for in the world outside our churches. Are we known as critics, consumers, copiers, condemners of culture? I'm afraid so. Why aren't we known as cultivators—people who tend and nourish what is best in human culture, who do the hard and painstaking work to preserve the best of what people before us have done? Why aren't we known as creators—people who dare to think and do something that has never been thought or done before, something that makes the world more welcoming and thrilling and beautiful?…
>
> So do you want to make culture? Find a community, a small group who can lovingly fuel your dreams and puncture your illusions. Find friends and form a family who are willing to see grace at work in one another's lives, who can discern together which

gifts and which crosses each has been called to bear. Find people who have a holy respect for power and a holy willingness to spend their power alongside the powerless. Find some partners in the wild and wonderful world beyond church doors.

And then, together, make something of the world.[4]

This is risk. This is obedience. This is kingdom living. This is Courageous Girls.

SHE TRUSTS AND OBEYS

The word *obey*, like the word *sin*, has a really bad reputation in today's culture. Unfortunately the word can be misconstrued and used to spiritually abuse people. But I want to make sure we consider the beauty and power in this word. Before I go any further, pause and consider the connotations you have with the word *obey*. Are they good? Are they bad? Do they make you want to close the book or skip this chapter? Me too. I am a bit stubborn and need to find my own way. So *obey* feels stifling, restricting, and even claustrophobic to me. Or it did before my epiphany that obedience is one of the roots of living fully.

I am a rule follower *for the most part*. My dad taught me, "Rules are for people who cannot make good decisions. When you cannot make a good decision, refer to the rule." That principle has surely given me pause in blindly following rules and has encouraged me to check in with the Holy Spirit to make a good decision. My desire to do the right thing comes out of a sense of not wanting to disappoint or cause trouble. That is the people pleaser in me. But God keeps putting me in situations where I feel as if I have to disappoint people in order to follow Him. It's really frustrating yet life altering at the same time. Obeying God is really hard for any human, even for a rule follower. Just because I want to do the "right thing" does not mean it's the "God thing," because it might not be what He is asking of me. Jesus was not exactly a rule follower. In fact, He bucked the system of His day in order to fulfill His mission. The Pharisees were not His fans, to say the least.

God has taught me how to move from being a people pleaser to being a woman of great faith, who obeys a God with a pretty remarkable plan. Three years ago at our mama retreat in central Oregon, we read the passage about Peter stepping out of the boat (see Matt. 14:22–33). I asked every woman to consider one way God was calling her to step out and to keep her eyes on Jesus and not her circumstances. It was powerful to listen to the different ways God was asking us to trust Him—not in foolish ways but in ways that required faith. That vulnerable moment of sharing with my Courageous Girls mamas started something in me. Our examples were diverse, unique to our own place in life but completely right for each of our stories.

When we are caught between fear and insecurity, life is pretty small. Risk-taking and acting on what we sense God leading us to do feels more like bondage than abundant life. About eight years ago, I was given the word *surrender* during a contemplative prayer retreat. It came just after Jeff and I launched our consulting and counseling business, Living Wholehearted. I did not know exactly what the word meant, but God would not let me move from that word for five years! Every year I would ask for another word with great anticipation, but I would sense I was not done with *surrender.* What does that say about me? Am I really that slow? Or did God know what He was doing? Hindsight is really twenty-twenty, and now I suspect He knew what He was doing.

In that five-year process, God was challenging my people-pleasing tendencies and forcing me to exercise my "No" muscle. I have helped many others with boundaries over the years and have recommended Lysa TerKeurst's book *The Best Yes* too many times to count.[5] However, God was calling me to deeper waters. To surrender one's will to God's will is one of the most risk-taking experiences in which a person can engage. Yet, as a follower of Jesus, I think it's one of the most life-altering and satisfying places I have ever been. On the front of my prayer journal years ago, I painted the word *surrender* with a tree trunk and the lyrics "Bending beneath the weight of His wind and mercy." Oh, how He loves us![6] Dreaming big and seeing those dreams come to fruition are my desires for every Courageous Mama and Girl. I'm not talking about just any dream but one birthed from the sacred spaces of intimacy with the God who loves and knows us like no other. That is fully living.

God finally gave me a new word ... well, two words actually: *trust* and *obey*. When those words came, I was a little nervous because I knew that He was asking me to start taking intentional risks. Thanks, Andy Crouch. I knew that the risks could not determine the outcome and that I would have to walk out on water without floating devices or safety nets. Only He could protect me and only He could take care of the consequences. Our job is to trust Him and commit our ways to Him. He does the rest. When obeying comes from a relationship rooted in love and grace, it really can feel like a no-brainer. And then at other times ... not so much. Sometimes trust requires the kind of leaning in to God that makes us feel as if we are learning to swim all over again—like the moment when the swim instructor asks us to float, trusting that the water will not swallow us alive. If you have ever had a swim lesson with your kid, you understand the fear that instruction can create. It's challenging to lie back in the water without any reservations!

However, once you do it, you are hooked. Psalm 37:3–7 says, "Trust in the LORD and do good; dwell in the land and cultivate faithfulness. Delight yourself in the LORD, and He will give you the desires of your heart. Commit your way to the LORD, trust also in Him, and He will do it. He will bring forth your righteousness as the light and your judgment as the noonday. Rest in the LORD and wait patiently for Him" (NASB). There is so much richness in these verses, but the key here is to note the ebb and flow between our part and His. We trust in Him, delighting in Him and committing our ways to Him, and let Him do the rest.

SHE ACCEPTS HER STARTING PLACE

Maybe dreaming comes naturally to you, or perhaps you tend to pop your own bubbles by unintentionally sabotaging or procrastinating on your dreams. Maybe dreaming feels impractical and irresponsible. Maybe, in your mind, dreaming is only for other women, whatever that means to you. In so many of our cases, trauma and abuse have destroyed our ability to dream. In some instances, staying in our trauma paradigm—where our fears keep us stuck—feels safe, so we become highly conservative and controlling and venture only into known waters. Fear of the unknown becomes the marker of our lives. In other cases, we become irrational and impulsive and do only what will take the pain immediately away. The natural consequences of abuse and trauma snatch our hope of tomorrow and cause us to prepare ceaselessly for the worst-case scenario. Trust and obedience seem too scary for someone who was deeply harmed, violated, or betrayed by someone she trusted.

I want you to know that our God is not abusive and will never violate our wills. He designed us for so much and will allow us to take as long as we need to heal. He is compassionate and patient.

There is grace for where we are today, and He will help us take one step at a time toward dreaming. Healing requires new thinking, new experiences, and new practices that repair our neural pathways in order for our bodies and guts to catch up. It will take time. For those who are unable to dream yet, we can walk alongside them as hope agents. Trauma can be healed, and the shame that paralyzes us can be lifted, but it requires time and consistent safe places to land before we can dream big. We all need to know someone can catch us when we fall. The step to get help and heal is an intentional risk. It could be your first!

There is grace for where you are, and I hope this chapter paints a picture of what could be for you and your daughter. Healing from our past is an essential ingredient to dreaming big. It requires one action step at a time in the present in order to affect the future and bring hope for tomorrow. Trust and obedience are the other ingredients. Just like our daughters, we must know that our Father in heaven is good and kind and loves us before we will obey. Obeying out of fear or obligation—or because we think He is angry or critical—produces nothing more than performance.

In King David's confession, Psalm 51, he said, "You do not delight in sacrifice, otherwise I would give it; You are not pleased with burnt offering. The sacrifices of God are a broken spirit; a broken and a contrite heart, O God, You will not despise" (vv. 16–17 NASB). God wants our whole hearts, not our sacrifices. Obedience without a heart smells fishy to God and, let's be honest, even to others. Sometimes we think we can fool people, but most can tell the difference between people being authentic in their good works and people who are just trying really hard. When we are able to heal, we can see that God is not abusive but only good. Obeying out of desire and a trusting relationship with God is the greatest risk of all and leads to quite an adventure. Missionaries are not the only ones who have a call on their lives. Moms all over the world are change agents in their spheres of influence.

Have you considered God's vision for you and your life? Does it extend beyond your next vacation or even the next soccer game? Maybe you are just trying to make ends meet or find time to sleep. I hear you, and I am not trying to add more to your plate. I just want you to know that God is at work in and through you and this life is meant for so much more than you or I can imagine.

There is grace for where you are, and you are right where you are supposed to be. Start here; start now. Ask God to show you the next step. When you do not know anything else to do, start with reading God's Word. Psalm 119:105 says, "Your word is a lamp for my feet, a light on my path." Start with where you are. Then He will part the waters and show you the way.

SHE REFLECTS HIS LOVE TO OTHERS

Obedience means people will know we belong to God. Jesus said, "By this everyone will know that you are my disciples, if you love one another" (John 13:35). First John 5:2–3 says, "By this we know that we love [or are] the children of God, when we love God and obey his commandments. For this is the love of God, that we keep his commandments. And his commandments are not burdensome" (ESV). His Word tells us how to live, but even more, His Spirit invites us into a personal journey with Him. Dreaming and allowing God to lead the way lead to a thrilling life.

God is not a genie who grants our every wish. However, *if* God is orchestrating His dream through us, it will happen. It surely does not always happen in the manner in which we think it will, and it will likely take some time and intention on our part. God's way often has side roads, off roads, and some apparent dead ends. The first way we know our dreams are aligned with God is through the grid of Scripture. God does not tell us anything contrary to what He has already declared in the Bible. So when someone tells me that God said to divorce his wife for another woman, I can refer to God's Word for clarification (Scripture makes clear that God would not tell us to do that; see Matt. 19:9). Second, God asks us to do things that bring us peace. That does not mean we will not have moments when we feel scared or nervous, but it does mean that deep down we have confident peace. If you have lived your whole life pleasing people and doing what is expected of you, then you might need slow and steady practice here. Usually, seeking the counsel of another person can help us discern if our leaning is from God, hormones, or something we ate. Finally, if it's God's direction or call, He will make it happen. It sounds too simple, but it is biblically true.

As we discern our dreams with God, remember that His ways do not always align with our timeline. Noah waited one hundred and twenty years before the boat he was building in faith would save his family's lives from the rains that he claimed would flood the earth. Moses was in the desert for forty years before he was called to lead the Israelites out of Egypt. Jesus didn't start His ministry until He was thirty. We do not have to strive to make His dreams in us come alive; our job is simply to trust and obey.

Let God do what He is good at—using ordinary people to do extraordinary things. There is nothing He cannot do. So allow yourself to dream. Then allow your daughter(s) to dream. Allow her to think beyond today and then step back and imagine what she would need to do or ask of God to take a step toward that dream. It's not the dreaming that is most important but the relationship with God and the building of our faith. Let's empower our daughters to dream and then be blown away by how they partner with God to participate in a greater cause.

SHE ACCEPTS SHE IS NEITHER PERFECT NOR BORING (THE TWO GO HAND IN HAND)

God uses humanity even when we continually make mistakes. Dreaming beyond our abilities leaves room for God's mighty power to move through our frailness. Brené Brown said, "Understanding the difference between healthy striving and perfectionism is critical to laying down the shield and picking up your life. Research shows that perfectionism hampers success. In fact, it's often the path to depression, anxiety, addiction, and life-paralysis."[7] Amen, sister! Perfectionism kills the minds, bodies, and souls of so many moms and daughters. Let's learn to embrace the messiness of a house, the awkward blunders of our children in public, the far-too-real moments in our marriages, and the many times we fumble over ourselves. Perfection is boring. Every risk-taker knows that failing is a part of the greater journey to success. So let's quit trying to be perfect. Malcolm Gladwell shared his research on a history of misfits, underdogs, and little guys.[8] He told how our limitations might be the very things that develops strength within us for a greater cause. For example, having dyslexia can develop other skill sets and attune our ability to navigate uncharted terrain. What we see as a mistake or imperfection, God sees as an opportunity and grows another muscle to be used on purpose.

Let go of the need to please others. Let go of the need to post on social media. Let go of the need to look a certain way. Let go of the need to know how it will all work out. Dreaming requires the ability to move forward even when the finished product is not fully in place. I get that it's easier said than done for most, but for those who need to practice the gift of being human, it's important to start by failing. Start small: let your daughter go to school in an outfit that does not match, or cancel a commitment without lying about why.

Instead, truthfully admit you overcommitted yourself and need a break. Start by not wearing makeup when you go to the store. Start by not showering and playing with your daughter instead. (Oh wait, that one might happen already if you have littles in the home!)

In any case, Brown reminded us, "To love someone fiercely, to believe in something with your whole heart, to celebrate a fleeting moment in time, to fully engage in a life that doesn't come with guarantees—these are risks that involve vulnerability and often pain.... I'm learning that recognizing and leaning into the discomfort of vulnerability teaches us how to live with joy, gratitude, and grace." On the other hand, *"Perfectionism is a self-destructive and addictive belief system that fuels this primary thought:* If I look perfect, live perfectly, and do everything perfectly, I can avoid or minimize the painful feelings of shame, judgment, and blame."[9]

We have already established that pain is essential in the human experience and we cannot feel the thrill of a full life without the despair of the valleys. You cannot turn off the negative emotions without turning off the positive ones too. So in dreaming big, we have the grand invitation to participate in a far-greater purpose than our comfort and success. Meeting our own needs, though God cares for those dearly, should not be our end goal. He is up to something far grander, and He asks you, me, and our daughters to walk with Him so that He can show us what that is. Like Lucy in *The Lion, the Witch and the Wardrobe*, we have to be willing to step through a door. We do not always know where that door will lead, but we do know that Aslan is always present in the process. Others may question our faith, like Peter and Susan. Some might even try to sabotage it, like Edmund. And then there will be some who are like the professor, who see beyond the ordinary with us.[10] Regardless, being a dreamer can lead others to healing, hope, and redemption in ways they could never see themselves.

Courageous Girls dream big and allow God to use them for His glory, whether we see the whole picture or not. We know it's really not about us or about producing anything. It's about a relationship in which God loves us so much that He wants to partner with us to reach the world one person at a time. Joining forces with a community of moms and daughters can help us have more courage as we encourage one another to move beyond the mundane darkness of life. I have watched every mom in our Courageous Girls group step into her dreams and find joy. Being a mom is one of the greatest callings in life, but we are not defined by the title. We are defined by our position with Christ. Therefore, our dreams are not our own. They are planted in us and grown through us by faith in a God who is ever constant and compassionate and who sees the greater needs in our world. Courage sees beyond our kitchen sinks and says yes to God's call. Trust and obey with me. The world needs a few more women stepping out of the boat and keeping our eyes on Jesus.

Takeaway

Write down five things you would love to do if there were no time constraints, money issues, or other responsibilities in your life. Write down five barriers that keep you from accomplishing those five dreams. Note that these are not necessarily the dreams God has for you, but it's a starting point to assess where you currently are in life and to see how God shapes your vision. Then read Psalm 37:3–7 and pray it over yourself and your daughter. It says, "Trust in the LORD…. Delight yourself in the LORD…. Commit your way to the LORD…. He will bring forth your righteousness…. Be still before the LORD and wait patiently for him" (ESV). Notice which word or phrase stands out to you the most. Then ask God to show you an action step that He is asking you to take related to that word or phrase.

Take It a Step Further

Memorize Ephesians 3:16–21 with your daughter. This is the founding verse behind Courageous Girls. Keep a journal to see how God uses these words to move in your life and the life of your daughter.

10

She Practices Rhythms of Rest

Most of us are more tired than we know at the soul level. We are teetering on the brink of dangerous exhaustion, and we really cannot do anything else until we have gotten some rest.... We really can't engage any [spiritual disciplines] until solitude becomes a place of rest for us rather than another place for human striving and hard work.

Ruth Haley Barton, *Sacred Rhythms*

Not all of us can do great things. But we can do small things with great love.

Mother Teresa

The gift of time and being fully present is rare these days. Sometimes all we long for as moms or daughters is just to *be*—to be together with no agenda, no demands, no lectures, and no expectations. In fact, being present is one of the three essential ingredients for a thriving relationship, both vertically and horizontally. As I mentioned in a previous chapter, the other two ingredients are *I have a voice* and *you have a voice*. Though it sounds so simple, the ability to be fully present is an advanced discipline and does not come easily to many. Most of the Courageous Girls curriculum is helping moms and daughters discover and practice these components of healthy relationships.

SHE EMBRACES THE MINISTRY OF PRESENCE

Not only does being present require us to engage our bodies, minds, and spirits, but it also requires that we let go of the past and the worries of tomorrow. Whew! That sounds like a tall order in Western culture in light of all the other concerns we've considered in this book. Shauna Niequist was right when she said, "The world will tell you how to live, if you let it. Don't let it. Take up your space. Raise your voice. Sing your song. This is your chance to make or remake a life that thrills you." She went on to say, "Present means we understand that the here and now is sacred, sacramental, threaded through with divinity even in its plainness. Especially in its plainness."[1] Tomorrow is not a guarantee, friend. And the more sober-minded we are, the more we know this to be true.

My husband, Jeff, was almost killed in a car accident his senior year of high school. This life-altering experience taught him two things: God is the main reason we are here, and all that is important is the present and the relationships in the current season. I have received wisdom from a man who knows that tomorrow can be taken away at the drop of a hat. He lives more fully present than most. You and I both know that life has a way of bringing many surprises. Recognizing that this moment might be the only one we have helps us reframe any situation.

I remember a moment many years ago when I was sitting on my couch: my living room was a mess, my kids were running around singing and dancing, and there was a pile of laundry about the size of Mount Everest next to me. In that moment I took a deep breath and could sense the Holy Spirit reminding me to just be present. I smelled the fresh laundry, listened to the piano as my youngest banged away on its keys, and watched my oldest (at the time only five) twirl in her little ballet tutu. The mess around me reminded me there was life. Life *abundant.* There was nothing profound or out of the ordinary, but something struck me deep in my soul with a whisper I have not forgotten—*This is life and it's good.*

A Courageous Girl is firmly rooted in gratitude and in the ability to be fully present and fully alive while holding tightly to Jesus in the midst of whatever is occurring around her. In order to have this perspective, we need regular rhythms in the Word, we need to check in with our souls, and we need to hear from the Lord. As Ecclesiastes reminds us, "There is a time for everything" (3:1). Tuning in to what is needed here and now is often the challenge. Let's explore the variety of ways we can practice rhythms of rest so that our daughters will be able to see the ebbs and flows of a healthy life in all its glorious plainness.

SHE ACCEPTS THE INVITATION TO REST

Opportunity has become an ever-present idol in the lives of our daughters. The cultural norm of making sure our kids do not miss out on anything—the best schooling, tutoring, music lessons, sports, camps, birthday parties, and more—is overwhelming. Moms are notorious for being the caretakers of the community; they are often the first to get up and the last to go to bed. Sometimes we can confuse rest for laziness or even selfishness. Add a little Jesus in the mix and we can feel convicted by false guilt to do more, be more, and fill our days with good things. Learning to slow down, spending time in quiet and solitude, is truly a discipline in discerning His voice for many of us moms who carry the weight of our worlds. In the midst of the noise around us—social media, news, work, school, coaches, church, marriages, kids, bills, and our own minds—times of solitude and self-care may sound like a luxury for most moms. However, for true transformation in our lives and in the lives of our daughters, rest is a necessity for those who want sustained health in their souls, relationships, and mothering.

We can model to our girls that life has rhythms; there's a time for work and a time for rest, a time for serving and a time for receiving, a time to be serious and a time to play. Not only will modeling rest help our girls be rooted in the gospel of grace; it will also help them live sustainable lives on the foundation of Christ. The messages that say "It's all up to me" or "I need to be responsible" or "No one will step up to the plate" can actually be detrimental to our spiritual journeys and create a lopsided way of living. Striving and always taking care of everyone and everything around us can zap joy and introduce all kinds of issues into our lives—such as codependency, selfishness, narcissism, bitterness, adrenal fatigue, burnout, health problems like IBS or headaches, anxiety, and depression. I cannot tell you how many women I hear say, "I want someone to take care of me for once!" If our daughters never see us take time with our God and for our own good, they will notice. Jesus said, "Love your neighbor as yourself" (Mark 12:31). If you do a poor job of loving yourself, the logic leads us to believe that you are doing a poor job of loving others. Ouch! One of my dear mentors reminded me that if your love for yourself is based on all you can accomplish and all you contribute to the world around you, then your expectations and love for others will also be based on what they can give you rather than on loving them as God's creation. Until we can understand how to love ourselves and others simply because we all exist, we will not be able to love others well.

Even Jesus, the God of the universe in the flesh, took time away from the crowds to be in solitude and relationship with His Father. Even Jesus needed to quiet the noise and be present with His heavenly Parent. Mark 1:34–37 says, "He healed many who were ill with various diseases, and cast out many demons; and He was not permitting the demons to speak, because they knew who He was. In the early morning, while it was still dark, Jesus got up, left the house, and went away to a secluded place, and was praying there. Simon and his companions searched for Him; they found Him, and said to Him, 'Everyone is looking for You'" (NASB). So when you sit down on the couch for a moment of peace to stare out the window and observe the beauty around you but your children immediately interrupt you, remember that you are in good company! Simon and all his companions searched for Jesus when He tried to be alone. So real, right? The truth is that being alone may not always work out, but nonetheless, we must recognize that it is essential to being a healthy Courageous Mama. We must learn to model rest and not the more common model of lopsided living (serve, do, give, do, crash).

SHE STAYS FOCUSED

What always strikes me about the Mark passage is the way that Jesus clearly knew where to go and what to do after He spent time with the Father. Jesus received direction in the quiet places, in prayer through exploring the sacred parts of the soul with His Father. At this time, many people had heard of Jesus' ability to heal, cast out demons, and preach good news. People were following Him (everywhere!), and despite their requests, the compassionate, loving, and merciful God in the flesh said, "Let us go somewhere else … so that I may preach there also; for that is what I came for" (v. 38 NASB). I can imagine that those people might have felt rejected, frustrated, or even angry. But Jesus was focused on His Father's business, not the people's agenda.

The pressure to say yes to the immediate and urgent needs before us keeps us from abundant life. Spending time checking in with our own souls, asking God to search us and tell us what He knows, confessing and aligning ourselves with Him, and listening for His voice happen when we pull away from the needs before us and allow ourselves to be still. A couple of times a year, we invite women out to the Living Wholehearted Lodge & Retreat for a day of contemplative prayer. These days of silence have become some of the most treasured and anticipated days because women need help slowing down.

SHE GOES TO JESUS TO FIND REST

I have meditated on Matthew 11:28–30 for years to remind my soul to go to the One who quenches my deepest thirst. *The Message* translation says that Jesus asked His disciples, "Are you tired? Worn out? Burned out on religion? Come to me. Get away with me and you'll recover your life. I'll show you how to take a real rest. Walk with me and work with me—watch how I do it. Learn the unforced rhythms of grace. I won't lay anything heavy or ill-fitting on you. Keep company with me and you'll learn to live freely and lightly." Jesus was speaking to the Israelites, who were burdened with a legalistic system and a long to-do list from the Pharisees. Their cultural expectations left them with guilt, frustration, and disappointment. Jesus offers us something completely apart from religiosity and the pressure to measure up to perfect standards. His grace invites us to enter rest. Rest is one of the most amazing aspects of a relationship with Christ because it means more than just sleeping. It is the kind of rest that means "it is well with my soul."[2]

The most profound idea of rest is found in Hebrews 3:7—4:11. God had worked and created for six days as He spoke the world into existence. God did not get tired, but He chose to lay down His work and call it good. I love that He did not call His work amazing, excellent, or even perfect. He called it *good* (see Gen. 1). Our attempts to innovate and improve are not for God's glory but for our own glory. That is such a humbling concept because God chose to rest and then offered us the gift to rest on the Sabbath. It's unfortunate that most of us will not receive the gift because we have too much to do.

Just like most idols, coveting our time can take the place of a relationship with God. Productivity and doing things for Jesus can become more of a focus for us than Jesus Himself. Martha knew what this is like as she slaved away in the kitchen while her sister, Mary, sat at the feet of Jesus. The dialogue between Martha and Jesus is fascinating: "'Lord, don't you care that my sister has left me to do the work by myself? Tell her to help me!' 'Martha, Martha,' the Lord answered, 'you are worried and upset about many things, but few things are needed—or indeed only one. Mary has chosen what is better, and it will not be taken away from her'" (Luke 10:40–42).

What is better? It is time with Jesus. It's not doing *for* Jesus but instead learning to be still and know that He is God (see Ps. 46:10). Martha was worrying about things that did not ultimately matter. It is important to help our children with homework and give them opportunities to explore their talents, experiences, and minds. However, when all is said and done, Millennials and Generation Z have more access to innovation due to their tech-savvy ways than any other previous generation. Some have said that they are more likely to be entrepreneurial, starting businesses in their early teens and having more degrees than generations prior. Yet I am not sure they are the most fulfilled. The soul that finds security in a relationship with Christ will be able to set boundaries, say no, take a Sabbath, and have a regular quiet time.

These are not legalistic tasks to accomplish but instead are practical ways to model to our children that life is not all about what we do but about who we do it with and why.

SHE STAYS IN TUNE WITH HER BODY

Another practical way we can find rest is by staying in tune with our bodies. As we learn that our bodies give us insight into what we need and how we feel, we do a better job of recognizing the rhythms we need to stay ahead of the curve. Often sickness, fatigue, moodiness, anxiety, depression, and other physical problems can be symptoms of stress and lack of rest, maybe even unresolved hurts. A good question to ask yourself is "What do I feel in my body right now?" If you do not know, then start by asking God to tell you. If you still do not know, you may be either numb or fully dissociated from your body. You have learned to live only in your "thinking brain" to avoid feeling; it is time to learn what is happening below the neck.

Many dysfunctional ways of living are birthed out of a disconnection from our bodies. We need to learn how to pay attention to our physical cues. Giving name to the level of intensity we feel in our bodies, even applying a scale from one to ten, will help us measure what our bodies need in the moment and keep us connected. When we pay attention to our bodies—similar to clumsy people in a Chihuly glass museum who have to think about where they walk and the pace at which they move (I might relate!)—peace is possible regardless of circumstance. When we ignore our bodies, we can guarantee something is going to break. Learning to tune in to our bodies and identify the level of intensity we are feeling in a particular area helps us prevent a flight, fight, or freeze response. It also prevents us from "flipping our lids," as Dr. Siegel suggested.[3] When our lids flip, we can guarantee that we are running only on fumes and that our bodies are experiencing copious amounts of stress hormones. The effects on us and those around us will eventually take their toll.

I am notorious for ignoring the dashboard on my car, and I have way too many stories where the ending was not so happy. Lesson learned: pay attention to the warning signs on the dashboard! Forging ahead when we are overworked, tired, and stressed should initiate internal sirens that tell us it's time to shift to a lower gear or maybe even hit the brakes. When our bodies are trying to function at a high level of intensity, it's as if our bodies' engines are catching on fire. The emotions we feel in our bodies (anxiety, anger, guilt, shame, grief, fear, etc.) can help us cue in to when it's time to pause, evaluate our needs, and find rest in the Lord. Sometimes our bodies communicate before our hearts, minds, and souls. Helping our daughters learn to regulate their emotions and body intensity is one of the key lessons in the Courageous Girls curriculum. However, in order for them to be able to self-regulate, we have to learn it first so that they can see it in action. Courageous Girls learn how to do this—not perfectly but well. My hope is that this type of mind-body awareness will be both yours and your daughter's normal before she reaches adulthood.

If you need help to find simple ways to rest and even schedule it in your day, here are some ideas:

1. Take a quiet time in the morning or evening.
2. Schedule a walk between meetings.
3. Take deep breaths to trick your brain into believing you are calm.
4. Schedule a half-day prayer retreat in a quiet location.

5. Go on a mini spa vacation in the bathtub or take a longer shower.
6. Revel in your five senses (sight, smell, hearing, taste, and touch) and enjoy the moment.
7. Exercise and allow your body to shift hormonally.
8. Try journaling (research truly backs this one up).
9. Stop multitasking and do one thing at a time at a slower pace.
10. Put on music and allow the words and the rhythm to calm your brain.

Three ways we can stay in tune with our bodies are exercising, eating well, and drinking water. So often we forget that self-care includes the basics, like going to the restroom when our bodies are actually cuing us to go. In all seriousness, this can be the most basic practice for moms and daughters. Just go to the bathroom! Life will continue if you take two minutes to excuse yourself. Drinking water and listening to hunger cues are other ways to grow in the rhythms of rest. This teaches our girls that being healthy is not about how we look but about how we feel. When food becomes a coping mechanism as a way either to control life or to numb life with quick fixes, we have misplaced its purpose. I have never been a fan of diets, mostly because I love all foods. However, I *am* a fan of listening to what our bodies need and crave. If you truly pay attention, you will be surprised to find that your body will tell you what it needs. The next time you go to the refrigerator or pantry, pause long enough to first see if you are hungry (and not bored, angry, sad, or lonely). Then check in with your tummy to see what sounds good. Protein? Dairy? Chocolate? Allowing food to be a fuel and not a good or evil will prevent our daughters from framing food as the enemy. In fact, food is a pleasure and a gift from the Lord. When it's in its rightful place, our bodies will naturally adjust to the right size for our own frame and God's design. Trying to be someone else's body shape is playing into the comparison game.

Finding rest in our body size—and in the food we consume—is truly half the battle. The final half of the battle is seeing movement and exercise as a way to process our emotions, clean out our organs, receive feel-good hormones, and maintain a sustainable body weight that helps us do good things with God. This is a process, and throughout many years of walking with women of every shape and size *and* being a woman of different shapes and sizes throughout many seasons, the greatest diet I have found is simply staying in tune with one's emotional health and what the body requests. Occasionally, I do crave a kale or spinach salad. I also crave burgers and fries. Since giving up dairy because of an intolerance in my digestive system, I rarely crave ice cream anymore. When we truly listen to what makes us feel good, we will find that our bodies adjust. Most of our body weight is related more to genes and emotional baggage. Yes, what we eat and how we exercise do affect our body sizes, but when those are the main focus, we will always find ourselves relapsing. Finding rest in whatever size we are and tuning in to the deeper needs of the soul and body will produce lasting change.

SHE CAN BE BORED AND UNPLUG

No matter what the day entails, you can encourage your daughter to take twenty to thirty minutes a day to be by herself and engage in something she wants to do. Maybe that means reading, playing with Legos, dancing, or playing with a pet. Do not get so fixated on a need to read the Bible or journal, though as she gets older, this rhythm is important to navigate. When our girls are younger, we might engage in quiet time with them in the mornings or evenings depending on our routines and lifestyle. In any case, the point is to integrate a way of being alone, without a device or performing a scheduled activity or chore, so that we can cultivate meaningful rest.

Sometimes our daughters might say they are bored when we create this kind of routine in our homes. Resist the temptation to rescue them from their struggle. Dr. Kevin Leman, a well-known psychologist and author in Christian circles, said that we need to let our children be bored, just as we need to feed them.[4] Tongue in cheek, he reminded us we are raising kids, not gerbils, so we need to get off the hamster wheel that perpetuates stressed-out homes. The Millennials (born 1981–1996) were the first generation in history to have a scheduled childhood, and the phenomenon has only become increasingly intense for their children. Whether you identify with the Millennials or Gen X, your way of doing life impacts whether or not your daughter sees a value in the rhythms of work, play, and rest.

Learning how to be bored, with no agenda or entertainment, is a fundamental life skill. A lack of ability to sit still, rest, find joy in the ordinary, or cultivate creativity without clear direction directly links to addictions, rigid thinking, and interference with intimate relationships. Not everything in our lives needs to be scheduled, entertaining, or productive. We are human *beings*, not human *doings*. Let's teach our daughters to be present by learning to be more present ourselves. Try pausing during the day to hug her for more than thirty seconds *just because*. Practice sitting still, or go for a walk and notice how creation reveals the nature of God.

Finally, take a moment and assess the level of involvement you have with your phone and other digital devices. If we are honest, most of us are addicted and compulsively look to see what else is happening outside this moment. Part of that problem has to do with a little pleasure hormone, dopamine, that is released every time we notice an incoming email, text, or call. The first rule of helping our daughters engage a digital world is managing our own. Scheduling on and off times for ourselves or taking longer to get back to someone via text can slow our Pavlovian responses. It has been clinically proven that technology increases anxiety, activates stress hormones, and creates forms of ADD-like symptoms. Because of increased levels of sensory overload, moms and daughters alike have shorter fuses and less tolerance for interruption, and they struggle to stand in line without looking at their phones. What happened to taking brief moments of inactivity to enjoy the smell of the air, take deep breaths, or look into our daughters' eyes? Another way we can manage our digital devices is engaging in downtime as a family, when each family member puts their devices in the same place and devotes the rest of the evening to family time. Not only will this calm everyone's brains, but your daughter also might actually talk with you and engage with you more regularly.

SHE PROTECTS HER WHITE SPACE

"White space" is the white margin on the edges of any paper.[5] It's the boundary between where a person writes on the lines and where the writing stops. I am guilty of writing in the white space whenever I take notes. I like the creativity and efficiency of packing one side of a note page full of good insights, flipping to the other side only if necessary. The downside is that I also do this in my life. Packing every hour of my day with important and good things to do feels efficient. However, wisdom would say to leave the edge of the paper and some space in my schedule just in case life takes a quick turn. (And we all know it can and it does.) Jamming our lives full of activities does not equate to a life well lived. I often get this question: "How do you do it all, Terra?" The truth is I don't. I have learned the art of delegation in how we run our businesses, ministries, personal Courageous Girls groups, and home life. I love to help others discover their gifts, talents, and contributions, while we cocreate together. It is not always efficient, but it surely is a helpful way to leave margin and see others experience their potential. Having our girls help around the house or help us get ready for a Courageous Girls meeting teaches them principles of shared responsibility, value for others, teamwork, and ownership.

I also have to practice time blocking by creating white space on my calendar. I have days and weekends with no scheduled plans, which allows me to be spontaneous and in the moment. No one else knows I am doing this apart from my family. Time blocking is similar to financial budgeting. Similar to how we save, give, and spend our money, we can plan and designate our time. Both are forms of resources. Try having a couple of nights a week with no sports, dinner dates, or church activities. It will leave room for relationship building. Maybe limit the number of activities for your daughter so that she can enjoy margin in her life. There is not a direct clinical correlation, but many anxieties and behavioral issues we see in our offices are partially due to children being overworked, overtired, and relationship-deprived. Children need margin just to be kids.

When we choose to leave white space in our routines, we find more moments when we can say yes to spontaneous requests from our daughters to play, read, or spend time with them. Margin gives us freedom to say yes to watching a movie together or cuddling a little longer at bedtime. As women, we know what it is like to make a spontaneous request to our husbands or friends. When they accept our offer to spend time together, it deposits something valuable into our love tanks. White space also gives us breathing room when emergencies happen. No one can plan for these, but leaving time between the larger tasks in our days, weeks, and months can be our saving grace. It seems a little ironic that we need to schedule time for boredom, spontaneity, or emergencies, but in many cases, it might be the only way we find the time.

SHE CARES FOR HERSELF AND PLAYS

Self-care comes in many forms and is unique to you. My self-care involves gardening, walking with friends, exercising, and journaling. What does your self-care look like? Can your daughter see you participating in self-care? Does she even know it exists? Are you modeling it to her in tangible ways and allowing her to have her own time for herself away from siblings, family, and the demands of school or activities? Let her be the motivation for you to start caring for yourself. Otherwise you are teaching your daughter how to be a caretaker at the expense of her own needs. *Codependency* is a label for those of us who live to make everyone else happy at the cost of our own health. Love is not codependent.

A destructive belief that I often hear about this topic is that "it's selfish to love myself." But Jesus said to love others as you love yourself (see Mark 12:31). God's Word beautifully illustrates a give-and-take relationship between the "I" and the "other." Grace is at the center of that tension. I love the moments in Scripture when Jesus received from others. When Jesus entered into His ministry, He spent forty days in the wilderness, where He fasted and was tempted by the enemy. Jesus resisted, and the devil fled. And then "angels came and attended him" (Matt. 4:11). We all know and think of Jesus as a giver, but He also received. Every Christmas we are reminded that the God of the universe came down from the heavens and became a baby. For many years Jesus was cared for and nurtured by Mary and Joseph. Learning how to receive is a powerful way for us to remember our humanity. And recognizing our humanity keeps us connected to the foundation of our faith—we have needs that can be met only by receiving. A few core needs include security, acceptance, significance, and hope. We also need to be seen, known, and loved. Self-care is a kinesthetic discipline. Even sleeping when tired will bear much fruit. Keeping the rhythm of give-and-take through our own self-care and meeting the needs of others helps us live in the tension of grace.

An all-or-nothing mind-set can signal performance-based faith and hidden trauma. ("I have to perform in order to be loved.") Self-care is part of loving ourselves well. We can liken it to the oxygen masks in an airplane. If you have ever flown on a plane, you know that passengers are taught to put on their oxygen masks before assisting others, including our children. Parenting is similar; we must make sure we have fueled our own bodies, souls, and minds in order to be helpful to our girls (and all the others who call on us). Self-care does not have to cost money. In fact, I would encourage you to keep it simple. The simpler it is, the more likely you will do it.

The Courageous Girls curriculum addresses ways to move beyond our own comfort to serve others. In fact, we encourage moms and daughters to practice this regularly. We wash one another's feet, make dates to get our hair and nails done, and take turns lifting up other moms and daughters with words of encouragement and prayers. But while serving, we must not neglect self-care. Try it yourself. Schedule regular times of getting away, sitting on the couch and staring out the window, taking a walk around the block, or curling up and reading a favorite book. Simply slowing down long enough to breathe in for four counts and slowly exhale for six counts can be life changing for many moms. There is no need to keep going, especially if your body is telling you it's reaching high intensity levels. These small ways of receiving invite us to participate in learning how to stay in the tension of loving others, just as we love ourselves or as God has loved us.

Self-care includes receiving care from others as well as learning how to play. Psychiatrist Stuart Brown, founder of the National Institute for Play in Carmel Valley, California, found that "play is a basic human need as essential to our well-being as sleep, so when we're low on play, our minds and bodies notice."[6] Based on our Core Values Index and family of origin, some of us engage in play easily. Others of us need to have play demonstrated because our whole lives have been about work, responsibility, and production. "What all play has in common," Brown said, "is that it offers a sense of engagement and pleasure, takes the player out of a sense of time and place, and the experience of doing it is more important than the outcome."[7] Sounds a little like grace to me—undeserved favor. We do not always have to earn time to play, but we do need time to play, laugh, engage with our daughters, enjoy our friendships, and create something simply for the sake of the art of creating. Play helps us recognize that life is about the process over the product and the effort rather than the outcome.

Play has been found to speed up learning, enhance productivity, and increase job satisfaction. Playing together in simple ways, like going to a concert, can enhance bonding and communication at home. Playful adults respond to stressors differently and seemingly with more ease. You might say that those who play have higher levels of resilience. Dr. Garry Landreth and other play-therapy experts said that play is to children what talking is to adults.[8] Play is the language of our daughters, and it allows them to process life. After 9/11, researchers found children processing through their play, crashing planes into the block towers they built. Adults do not need to process in this way, and playing *all* the time is not the point. The point is, we should not dismiss the power of play as it benefits you, your daughter, and your connection to God. Recall some of the things you enjoyed as a kid, and allow yourself to try them again. Play hopscotch. Play dress-up with your daughter. Order off the kids' menu and get a prize. What is holding you back from play? Take a moment to ponder your ability to play and consider how you might try to today.

SHE EMBRACES THE ORDINARY MOMENTS

Over the years as *American Idol, The Voice,* and *So You Think You Can Dance* have become our new realities, I have noticed that the temptation to sensationalize everything we do is hindering our joy and our contentment. We think we can or must go from being a stay-at-home mom to a YouTube sensation by recording everything we do and posting it for all to see. Personally, I do not want you to peep into my life. Privacy, solitude, and downtime have become more valuable than gold.

For years, I chose not to engage in social media because I knew my tendency to compare myself to others and I saw the potential urge to strive for something outside my personal call from God. This was my own conviction, and there is no judgment on yours. Now that I am an author, I have had to reconsider my stance on social media and have been growing new muscles. The temptations are still there, but I have strong boundaries in place, good accountability, and a clear purpose. For example, I do not scroll late at night or on Sundays when I am trying to be present with my family. I have chosen to post only what seems to be aligned with the message of grace, hope, and encouragement for others. I also intentionally do not follow people who cause me more inward struggle.

As you think about social media, consider your limits. What helps you stay content where God has placed you? What causes you to stir internally and externally?

In God's economy, extraordinary living can look a little old school, especially if we put the standard up against the world's standard. The heroes of our faith are the individuals who put one foot in front of the next and did *only* what God was asking of them in the moment. Mother Teresa is one of my heroes. She realized that by loving one person at a time and helping them die with dignity, she could change the world. Her desire to do something big was fulfilled in the simple love of caring for those right in front of her. She got it. She did not have a platform on social media, yet the world heard about her over time as she was faithful in the small things. "Whoever can be trusted with very little can also be trusted with much, and whoever is dishonest with very little will also be dishonest with much" (Luke 16:10). Mother Teresa took this verse to heart. This quote is often attributed to her: "Be faithful in small things, because it is in them that your strength lies." She also said, "We ourselves feel that what we are doing is just a drop in the ocean. But if that drop was not in the ocean, I think the ocean would be less because of the missing drop."[9] Our contributions matter to God, whether it's praying for people, making them meals, changing their diapers, or looking them in the eye. We need to recognize that nothing is too small or too ordinary in God's kingdom. He sees you and values what you bring to Him. You are the contribution.

There are simple ways you can let your daughter know you value ordinary moments, such as letting her interrupt you occasionally when on a phone call or in the middle of a task. Pause what you're doing and look her in the eye. Let her know she is more important. Or if she asks for your attention, drop what you are doing and go to her. Sit with her and engage in her ordinary world when she invites you to be with her. Or take her for a walk with no other agenda but to spend time together. The ordinary monthly meetings where moms and daughters gather to pray, read and discuss the Word, do a craft, and talk can be some of the moments when she feels your love the most. These regular drops of time, attention, and intentional love speak louder than our words. Maybe spend time every night just lying with her and letting her talk, perhaps by identifying a high and low from her day. These are things that are mentioned at memorials, on Mother's Day, and when our children leave the house when they are grown. At the end of our lives, these are the moments—not the accomplishments or accolades—we wish we could get back.

When I was an undergrad, I took a ministry course that helped us navigate our specific passions in life. I will never forget when I heard the professor declare, "Your life is your ministry." It blew my mind. *You mean being me is enough for God and His kingdom purposes?* I have unpacked that simple truth over the years, and I still stand firm on it after twenty years. Having the courage to be myself allows me to minister to anyone before me. This seems too simple to be real, but it's the true message of grace. More than anything, God wants our whole hearts. We can truly rest in that.

Courageous Mama, you are loved. You are seen. You have a purpose. You are invited into intimate relationships with God and others. You are allowed to make mistakes and they can be redeemed. You can rest and allow God to move. You are invited to partner with His power to do more than you can ask or imagine (see Eph. 3:20). It's time to awaken our senses and recognize the times. Do not be caught up in the whirlwind of panic or dismissal that is common to the world, but take hold of the power we have been given by our God. He is in us. He is around us. He has gone before us. He is behind us. And He is the One on whom we stand—with confidence, resilience, and grace.

Our daughters are crying out for women to show them the way; they need us to lead. Imagine a generation of girls who know they are loved and who love others well. Imagine a generation of girls who speak life and encouragement and hope into those around them. Imagine a generation of girls who stand up not only for their own value and worth but also for the value and worth of others. Imagine a generation of girls who lean in to the mighty power of our God and live into their destiny—the one crafted for them for such a time as this!

The process of becoming a Courageous Girl requires knowing who we are in a community that practices moving through conflict rather than around it, calling us to deeper waters where we find intimacy with God and others. It requires surrender, trust, and obedience. All our journeys are never exactly how we envisioned them, but we can surely rest easy knowing that our God is in the business of restoring, renewing, and rebuilding the long devastation of past generations. Be on the alert and stand firm in the faith; be courageous and be strong. Let all that you do be done in love by His power. The time is now. Are you with me?

> I pray that out of his glorious riches he may strengthen you with power through his Spirit in your inner being, so that Christ may dwell in your hearts through faith. And I pray that you, being rooted and established in love, may have power, together with all the Lord's holy people, to grasp how wide and long and high and deep is the love of Christ, and to know this love that surpasses knowledge—that you may be filled to the measure of all the fullness of God.
>
> Now to him who is able to do immeasurably more than all we ask or imagine, according to his power that is at work within us, to him be glory in the church and in Christ Jesus throughout all generations, for ever and ever! Amen. (Eph. 3:16–21)

Takeaway

Write a list of five ordinary moments with your daughter this last month. Praise God for those moments and recognize the gift they have been to you. Also, try a technology fast with your daughter (you determine the amount of time). Journal about your experiences. What was difficult for you? What did you learn about yourself, about others, and about God? Did God reveal anything specific to you? Consider making this technology fast a part of the rhythm in your life.

Take It a Step Further

Schedule a half-day prayer session. Maybe connect with another mom and go together—not to talk but to have accountability for the time. Journal, listen, read, walk, and breathe deeply. Engaging in art, like making a collage, can often help the mind and body settle first. If you are up for a bigger challenge, schedule four of these retreats each year. Not only will this be a way to model to your daughter how you take time with God, but it will also help you pause, reflect, and stay on track with where He is leading you apart from all the other expectations coming your way.

Starting a Courageous Girls Group

The hardest part of starting anything is … starting. So congratulations! By reading *Courageous*, you have stepped over the line, and something is drawing you to begin a Courageous Girls group for your daughter. You are worth it. She is worth it.

We have provided you with everything you will need along the way at mycourageousgirls.com and it's *free*. With over one hundred lessons, ranging on everything from social media to sex, the Courageous Girls curriculum helps moms navigate every developmental stage of their growing daughters' lives. The only thing missing is your unique fingerprint, along with the other moms and daughters in your sphere of influence.

Starting and leading a Courageous Girls group does not mean you will have to host each time or lead each lesson. In fact, as a busy mom who was passionate about raising up other leaders, I designed Courageous Girls curriculum so that every mom-daughter pair you invite into your group will lead at least one lesson a year. Leading simply means you will be the one who invites, initiates, and delegates along the way. And by only having one meeting a month, most—if not all—moms can find a way to attend, showing their daughters that they are worth the time and effort.

With prayerful consideration, begin by asking whom God has already put in your sphere of influence and who in your community wants to grow in their own walk with God as they walk the road of motherhood. Take time to read through the website and explore the lessons. Every lesson intertwines with the truths in this book and aligns with the developmental level of your daughter. You will grow as she grows closer to God, to you, and to others in your group. Just by your reading this page, God is already working in you!

As you sink into trusting God each step of the way, believing He is with you, going before you, and empowering you to be a catalyst for transforming relationships, the Courageous Girls team is right beside you as your coach! For those who would like more in-depth coaching, we have a team of qualified coaches, videos, training, and podcasts. You've got this. On the website there are questions and answers for you to consider. Feel free to browse that section to become familiar with some of the roadblocks some moms experience.

Then send out an invitation for an initial gathering and see which moms say yes! This is not about doing it "right," but about learning how to lean in to and trust the One who knows you and those in your group so well. Get ready for an adventure.

GO IN TWOS

Jesus was strategic in sending out disciples two by two (see Luke 10:1). There is biblical wisdom and courage in partnering with another mom who will lead alongside you. Not only will you be able to share your initial responsibilities in the group, but you will also be modeling community and cocreating from the start. Ecclesiastes 4:9–10 says, "Two are better than one, because they have a good return for their labor: If either of them falls down, one can help the other up." I love the practicality of God's Word. Leadership can be hard in and of itself, and leading women has many of its own unique challenges. Consider someone to partner with you. Who comes to mind as you pray?

Maybe the mom with whom you partner is someone you do not know well but is someone with a different wiring or skill set that will meet the needs of your group over time. Or perhaps this mom is a close friend whom you trust and know will go the long haul with you based on your history together. Either way, make sure you ask God who *He* thinks is the one who should lead with you, and listen to His still voice. Then take intentional risk.

Whether you choose to go two by two or step out on your own, someone will have to make decisions for the group along the way. Every group of sheep needs a shepherd to keep the sheep from wandering aimlessly. Leadership is necessary for every community, so trying to avoid this role is not a good idea. Leadership with integrity is even more essential, and you will find that God will use your obedient yes to grow you, your faith, and your relationship with your daughter as she watches you step out to start this group with her in mind!

NOW WHAT?

Once you have prayed about a coleader, begin praying about who in your community loves Jesus or has a desire to grow in their spiritual journeys alongside their daughters. Read through the variety of links on mycourageousgirls.com to get acquainted with the mission of Courageous Girls and sample a few lessons. Women at all stages of their journeys are welcome to join and watch how God moves.

Once you have commitments from moms, it is ideal to have them read this book prior to launching your group, perhaps as a group, as a way to go deeper in relationship. Having an additional book study together with prayer and dialogue will only help you go deeper together.

It's time to stand up for your daughter and lead her well. There is no better way to do this than with other moms and daughters over the course of a long, committed journey. This is where being wrapped *in courage* really counts. God is with you.

If You Enjoyed This Book

If *Courageous* has made an impact on you, consider taking additional steps to further your own journey and help other women grow as well. Read through the following options, and pray as you consider committing to one, two, or even all five.

1. Follow me (Terra Mattson) on Instagram and subscribe to my podcast called *Living Wholehearted Podcast with Jeff and Terra Mattson*. Take a step further and tell us about your story and the impact *Courageous* has had on you. We would be honored to receive an email, a social media message, or a one- to two-minute video from you.

2. Invite five to eight women to form a book study with you. Read *Courageous* together; it will help you move deeper into community with these other women, and you'll find new takeaways by reading it again.

3. Study *Courageous* with your mom, sisters, or daughters (even if they are adults), allowing God to grow—and if needed, mend—your relationship.

4. Give a copy of *Courageous* to a mom you know who is raising a daughter or needs a reminder of her own value.

5. Dive deeper into your own story by starting your counseling journey. Visit livingwholehearted.com or mycourageousgirls.com for recommendations of counselors in your area.

Scriptures about Identity

2 Corinthians 5:17 ESV
"If anyone is in Christ, he is a new creation. The old has passed away; behold, the new has come."

1 Peter 2:9 ESV
"You are a chosen race, a royal priesthood, a holy nation, a people for his own possession, that you may proclaim the excellencies of him who called you out of darkness into his marvelous light."

Galatians 2:20 ESV
"I have been crucified with Christ. It is no longer I who live, but Christ who lives in me. And the life I now live in the flesh I live by faith in the Son of God, who loved me and gave himself for me."

John 15:15 ESV
"No longer do I call you servants, for the servant does not know what his master is doing; but I have called you friends, for all that I have heard from my Father I have made known to you."

John 1:12 ESV
"To all who did receive him, who believed in his name, he gave the right to become children of God."

Romans 8:17 ESV
"If children, then heirs—heirs of God and fellow heirs with Christ, provided we suffer with him in order that we may also be glorified with him."

Colossians 3:3 ESV
"You have died, and your life is hidden with Christ in God."

Galatians 3:26 ESV
"In Christ Jesus you are all sons of God, through faith."

Romans 8:1 ESV
"There is therefore now no condemnation for those who are in Christ Jesus."

Philippians 3:20 ESV
"Our citizenship is in heaven, and from it we await a Savior, the Lord Jesus Christ."

1 Corinthians 12:27 ESV
"You are the body of Christ and individually members of it."

1 Corinthians 6:19–20 ESV
"Do you not know that your body is a temple of the Holy Spirit within you, whom you have from God? You are not your own, for you were bought with a price. So glorify God in your body."

Ephesians 2:10 ESV
"We are his workmanship, created in Christ Jesus for good works, which God prepared beforehand, that we should walk in them."

Ephesians 4:24 ESV
"To put on the new self, created after the likeness of God in true righteousness and holiness."

John 3:16 ESV
"For God so loved the world, that he gave his only Son, that whoever believes in him should not perish but have eternal life."

Notes

INTRODUCTION

1. John Lynch, Bruce McNicol, and Bill Thrall, *The Cure: What If God Isn't Who You Think He Is and Neither Are You?* (Phoenix, AZ: Trueface, 2016), 3.

2. Peggy Orenstein, *Girls & Sex: Navigating the Complicated New Landscape* (New York: HarperCollins, 2017), 3.

3. Richard Weissbourd et al., *The Talk: How Adults Can Promote Young People's Healthy Relationships and Prevent Misogyny and Sexual Harassment*, Making Caring Common Project, Harvard Graduate School of Education, May 2017, https://mcc.gse.harvard.edu/thetalk.

4. Kelly Wallace, "Kids as Young as 5 Concerned about Body Image," CNN, February 13, 2015, www.cnn.com/2015/02/13/living/feat-body-image-kids -younger-ages/index.html.

5. This is a regular saying of Bill's. For more on this topic, see Bill Thrall et al., *The Cure & Parents* (San Clemente, CA: CrossSection, 2016).

6. William Wilberforce, "William Wilberforce Quotes," All the Best Quotes, accessed July 22, 2019, https://chatna.com/william-wilberforce-quotes/.

CHAPTER 1

1. Brené Brown, *I Thought It Was Just Me (but It Isn't): Making the Journey from "What Will People Think?" to "I Am Enough"* (New York: Avery, 2007), xxiii–xxiv.

2. Rudolf Bultmann, *Theology of the New Testament*, trans. Kendrick Grobel (Waco, TX: Baylor University Press, 2007), 1:220–22; Robert Jewett, *Paul's Anthropological Terms: A Study of Their Use in Conflict Settings* (Leiden,

Netherlands: E. J. Brill, 1971), 305–13; Hans Walter Wolff, *Anthropology of the Old Testament*, trans. Margaret Kohl (Philadelphia: Fortress, 1974), 40–58.

3. Max Lucado, *You Are Special* (Wheaton, IL: Crossway, 1997).

4. For more from Caroline Leaf, I recommend her book *Switch On Your Brain: The Key to Peak Happiness, Thinking, and Health* (Grand Rapids, MI: Baker, 2013).

5. Sue C. Bratton et al., *Child Parent Relationship Therapy (CPRT) Treatment Manual: A 10-Session Filial Therapy Model for Training Parents* (New York: Routledge, 2006), 50.

CHAPTER 2

1. Harville Hendrix, *Getting the Love You Want: A Guide for Couples* (New York: Henry Holt, 2001), xix.

2. John Ortberg, "In Between Despair and Joy," FaithGateway, April 18, 2019, www.faithgateway.com/in-between-despair-and-joy/#.Ww4YDJPwZE4.

3. Francesca Battistelli, vocalist, "If We're Honest," by Francesca Battistelli, Jeff Pardo, and Molly Reed, track 8 on *If We're Honest*.

4. Sue C. Bratton et al., *Child Parent Relationship Therapy (CPRT) Treatment Manual: A 10-Session Filial Therapy Model for Training Parents* (New York: Routledge, 2006), 7.

CHAPTER 3

1. Brené Brown, "The Power of Vulnerability" (TED Talk, TedxHouston, Houston, TX, June 2010), www.ted.com/talks/brene_brown_on_vulnerability.

2. Leonard Sax, *Why Gender Matters: What Parents and Teachers Need to Know about the Emerging Science of Sex Differences*, 2nd ed. (New York: Harmony Books, 2017), 86–88.

3. Melody Beattie, *Codependent No More: How to Stop Controlling Others and Start Caring for Yourself*, 2nd ed. (Center City, MN: Hazelden, 1992).

4. Tina Payne Bryson and Daniel J. Siegel, *The Whole-Brain Child: 12 Revolutionary Strategies to Nurture Your Child's Developing Mind* (New York: Bantam, 2012).

5. Milan and Kay Yerkovich, *How We Love: Discover Your Love Style, Enhance Your Marriage*, expanded ed. (Colorado Springs: WaterBrook, 2017), 16–17.

6. Daniel Siegel, "Flipping Your Lid," September 11, 2011, video, 7:27, www.heartmindonline.org/resources/daniel-siegel-flipping-your-lid.

7. Bessel van der Kolk, *The Body Keeps the Score: Brain, Mind, and Body in the Healing of Trauma* (New York: Penguin, 2014).

8. Shauna Niequist, *Present Over Perfect: Leaving Behind Frantic for a Simpler, More Soulful Way of Living* (Grand Rapids, MI: Zondervan, 2016), 85.

9. Gregory L. Jantz and Ann McMurray, *Hope, Help, and Healing for Eating Disorders: A Whole-Person Approach to Treatment of Anorexia, Bulimia, and Disordered Eating*, rev. ed. (Colorado Springs: WaterBrook, 2010), 176–77.

CHAPTER 4

1. C. S. Lewis, "Is Theology Poetry?," in *The Weight of Glory: And Other Addresses* (New York: HarperOne, 2001), 140.

2. Laura Flynn McCarthy, "What Babies Learn in the Womb," Parenting.com, accessed July 17, 2019, www.parenting.com/article/what-babies-learn -in-the-womb.

3. Malcolm Gladwell, *Outliers: The Story of Success* (New York: Little, Brown and Company, 2008), 41.

4. For more from these amazing mentors of mine, see John Lynch, Bruce McNicol, and Bill Thrall, *The Cure: What If God Isn't Who You Think He Is and Neither Are You?* (Phoenix, AZ: Trueface, 2016).

5. Kerry Dearborn (class lecture in *Women in Christianity*, Seattle Pacific University, Seattle, WA, 1999).

6. Ashley Turner, "Meditation 101: The Neuroscience of Why Meditation Works," *HuffPost*, April 3, 2017, www.huffingtonpost.com/ashley-turner/how -meditation-works_b_4702629.html.

7. William Sieber (lecture in Calming an Overactive Brain workshop, Institute for Brain Potential, Portland, OR, 2017).

8. Sally Lloyd-Jones, *The Jesus Storybook Bible: Every Story Whispers His Name* (Grand Rapids, MI: Zonderkidz, 2007), 36.

9. "Strong's H2580—Chen," Blue Letter Bible, accessed September 21, 2019, www.blueletterbible.org/lang/lexicon/lexicon.cfm?t=kjv&strongs=h2580; "Strong's G5485—Charis," Blue Letter Bible, accessed September 21, 2019, www.blueletterbible.org/lang/lexicon/lexicon.cfm?t=kjv&strongs=g5485.

10. Bill Thrall et al., *The Cure & Parents* (San Clemente, CA: CrossSection, 2016), 16, 18.

11. Brené Brown, *Daring Greatly: How the Courage to Be Vulnerable Transforms the Way We Live, Love, Parent, and Lead* (New York: Gotham, 2012), 68–69.

CHAPTER 5

1. Lexico, s.v. "drama," accessed September 21, 2019, www.lexico.com/en /definition/drama.

2. Les and Leslie Parrott often say this. For more on this, see Les Parrott and Leslie Parrott, *Saving Your Marriage Before It Starts: Seven Questions to Ask Before— and After—You Marry* (Grand Rapids, MI: Zondervan, 2015).

3. Hillsong UNITED, "Oceans (Where Feet May Fail)," by Joel Houston, Matt Crocker, and Salomon Ligthelm, track 4 on *Zion*, Hillsong Church, 2013.

4. See Bill Thrall et al., *The Cure & Parents* (San Clemente, CA: CrossSection, 2016).

5. Eric Metaxas said this at a conference, explaining it was the premise he wanted to express in his book, *Seven Women: And the Secret of Their Greatness* (Nashville: Nelson, 2015).

6. See Archibald D. Hart and Sylvia Hart Frejd, *The Digital Invasion: How Technology Is Shaping You and Your Relationships* (Grand Rapids, MI: Baker, 2013).

7. Spencer Van Dyk, "Humans Only Able to Maintain Five Relationships in Their Inner-Circle, 150 in Their Outer-Circle: Study," *National Post*, May 3, 2016, http://nationalpost.com/news/world/humans-only-able-to-maintain-five -relationships-in-their-inner-circle-and-150-in-their-outer-circle-study-finds.

8. Beth Moore, *So Long, Insecurity: You've Been a Bad Friend to Us* (Carol Stream, IL: Tyndale, 2010).

9. Strong's H3045—Yada," Blue Letter Bible, accessed September 22, 2019, www.blueletterbible.org/lang/lexicon/lexicon.cfm?Strongs=H3045&t=KJV.

10. Katy Steinmetz, "Beyond 'He' or 'She': The Changing Meaning of Gender and Sexuality," *Time*, March 16, 2017, https://time.com/4703309/gender -sexuality-changing.

11. Liz Mineo, "Good Genes Are Nice, but Joy Is Better," *Harvard Gazette*, April 11, 2017, https://news.harvard.edu/gazette/story/2017/04/over-nearly-80 -years-harvard-study-has-been-showing-how-to-live-a-healthy-and-happy-life/.

12. Harville Hendrix, *Getting the Love You Want: A Guide for Couples* (New York: Henry Holt, 2001), xix.

13. Dietrich Bonhoeffer, *Life Together*, trans. John W. Doberstein (London: SCM, 2015), 57–58.

14. Brené Brown, *Daring Greatly: How the Courage to Be Vulnerable Transforms the Way We Live, Love, Parent, and Lead* (New York: Gotham, 2012), 53.

15. Henry Cloud, *The Law of Happiness: How Spiritual Wisdom and Modern Science Can Change Your Life* (New York: Howard, 2012), 129. For an additional resource, I recommend Henry Cloud and John Townsend, *Boundaries When to Say Yes, How to Say No to Take Control of Your Life*, rev. ed. (Grand Rapids, MI: Zondervan, 2017).

16. See Sue C. Bratton et al., *Child Parent Relationship Therapy (CPRT) Treatment Manual: A 10-Session Filial Therapy Model for Training Parents* (New York: Routledge, 2006).

CHAPTER 6

1. Alistair Begg, "Genuine Love Takes Initiative," *Truth for Life* (blog), April 18, 2017, https://blog.truthforlife.org/genuine-love-takes-initiative.

2. "What Is the Core Values Index?," Taylor Protocols, accessed July 18, 2019, www.taylorprotocolsinc.com/how-the-cvi-works.

3. Daniel J. Canary and Susan J. Messman, "Relationship Conflict," in *Close Relationships: A Sourcebook*, ed. Clyde Hendrick and Susan S. Hendrick (Thousand Oaks, CA: Sage, 2000), 261.

4. John M. Gottman and Nan Silver, *The Seven Principles for Making Marriage Work: A Practical Guide from the Country's Foremost Relationship Expert* (New York: Harmony Books, 2015), 1–2.

5. Gottman and Silver, *Seven Principles*, 32–39.

6. Gottman and Silver, *Seven Principles*, 27.

7. Timothy Keller, "Hope Beyond the Walls of the World: A Christian View of the Problem of Hope and the Purpose of Story" (lecture, University of Hong Kong, Hong Kong, March 22, 2014), www.youtube.com/watch?time_continue=2668&v=SD5LYJ3us0U.

8. See Bill Thrall, Bruce McNicol, and John Lynch, *Behind the Mask: Reversing the Process of Unresolved Life Issues* (Phoenix, AZ: Leadership Catalyst, 2005), 19–20.

9. Sue C. Bratton et al., *Child Parent Relationship Therapy (CPRT) Treatment Manual: A 10-Session Filial Therapy Model for Training Parents* (New York: Routledge, 2006), 7.

10. Dictionary.com, s.v. "conflict," accessed July 18, 2019, www.dictionary.com /browse/conflict.

11. Henry Cloud, *Necessary Endings: The Employees, Businesses, and Relationships That All of Us Have to Give Up in Order to Move Forward* (New York: HarperBusiness, 2010).

12. Ruth Haley Barton, *Sacred Rhythms: Arranging Our Lives for Spiritual Transformation* (Downers Grove, IL: InterVarsity, 2006), 105.

13. Jean Decety and William Ickes, eds., *The Social Neuroscience of Empathy* (Cambridge, MA: MIT Press, 2009).

14. "Strong's G863—Aphiēmi," Blue Letter Bible, accessed September 23, 2019, www.blueletterbible.org/lang/lexicon/lexicon.cfm?t=kjv&strongs=g863.

15. Steven R. Tracy, *Mending the Soul: Understanding and Healing Abuse* (Grand Rapids, MI: Zondervan, 2005) 180–94.

16. See mycouragourageousgirls.com for definitions of abuse.

17. To explore your own CVI, go to livingwholehearted.com or read more on mycourageousgirls.com, third year curriculum.

CHAPTER 7

1. Beth Moore, *Esther: It's Tough Being a Woman* (Nashville: LifeWay, 2008), 107–8.

2. Gavin de Becker, *The Gift of Fear: And Other Survival Signals That Protect Us from Violence* (New York: Dell, 1997).

3. Karen Reivich and Andrew Shatté, *The Resilience Factor: 7 Keys to Finding Your Inner Strength and Overcoming Life's Hurdles* (New York: Broadway, 2003), 3–4, 11.

4. Katherine Wolf and Jay Wolf, *Hope Heals: A True Story of Overwhelming Loss and Overcoming Love* (Grand Rapids, MI: Zondervan, 2016), 164–65.

5. David D. Burstein, *Fast Future: How the Millennial Generation Is Shaping Our World* (Boston: Beacon, 2013).

6. Christopher Wilson, Kimberly A. Lonsway, and Joanne Archambault, *Understanding the Neurobiology of Trauma and Implications for Interviewing Victims*, (Colville, WA: End Violence Against Women International, November 2016), www.evawintl.org/Library/DocumentLibraryHandler.ashx?id=842.

7. Sue C. Bratton et al., *Child Parent Relationship Therapy (CPRT) Treatment Manual: A 10-Session Filial Therapy Model for Training Parents* (New York: Routledge, 2006), 53–56.

CHAPTER 8

1. A sexual time line is a linear account of experiences that formed your views of gender, sexuality, and the relationship between the two.

2. See Peggy Orenstein, *Girls & Sex: Navigating the Complicated New Landscape* (New York: HarperCollins, 2017), 8, 54.

3. Orenstein, *Girls & Sex*, 19.

4. Orenstein, *Girls & Sex*, 165.

5. Philip G. Zimbardo and Nikita Duncan, *The Demise of Guys: Why Boys Are Struggling and What We Can Do about It* (New York: TED Conferences, 2012).

6. Archibald D. Hart and Sylvia Hart Frejd, *The Digital Invasion: How Technology Is Shaping You and Your Relationships* (Grand Rapids, MI: Baker, 2013).

7. Leonard Sax, *Why Gender Matters: What Parents and Teachers Need to Know about the Emerging Science of Sex Differences* (New York: Harmony Books, 2017), 11–12.

8. Jonathan Haidt and Lenore Skenazy, "The Fragile Generation," *Reason*, December 2017, https://reason.com/2017/10/26/the-fragile-generation/.

9. *Moana*, directed by Ron Clements and John Musker (Burbank, CA: Walt Disney Pictures, 2016).

10. Linda Dillow and Lorraine Pintus, *Intimate Issues: 21 Questions Christian Women Ask about Sex* (Colorado Springs: WaterBrook, 1999), 9.

11. Orenstein, *Girls & Sex*, 3.

12. Richard Weissbourd et al., *The Talk: How Adults Can Promote Young People's Healthy Relationships and Prevent Misogyny and Sexual Harassment*, Making Caring Common Project, Harvard Graduate School of Education, May 2017, https://mcc.gse.harvard.edu/thetalk.

13. Kelly Wallace, "Kids as Young as 5 Concerned about Body Image," CNN, February 13, 2015, www.cnn.com/2015/02/13/living/feat-body-image-kids -younger-ages/index.html.

14. Regulating one's sexuality is a key component of the sex addiction recovery work I have been doing for years with couples. If men and women have never taken time to find healthy ways to meet their legitimate, God-given needs for emotional intimacy, they will experience anger, disconnection, stress, and loneliness. If their legitimate needs are not met, they will try to meet them in illegitimate ways by turning to patterns that are dangerous and destructive for the brain such as masturbation, pornography, and extramarital affairs.

15. Dictionary.com, s.v. "modest," accessed July 18, 2019, www.dictionary.com /browse/modest.

16. A sexual time line is a linear account of experiences that formed your views of gender, sexuality, and the relationship between the two.

CHAPTER 9

1. C. S. Lewis, "Is Theology Poetry?," in *The Weight of Glory: And Other Addresses* (New York: HarperOne, 2001), 140.

2. C. S. Lewis, *The Screwtape Letters* (New York: HarperCollins, 2001).

3. Andy Crouch, *Strong and Weak: Embracing a Life of Love, Risk & True Flourishing* (Downers Grove, IL: InterVarsity, 2016), 41.

4. Andy Crouch, *Culture Making: Recovering Our Creative Calling* (Downers Grove, IL: InterVarsity, 2008), 57, 97–98, 263.

5. Lysa TerKeurst, *The Best Yes: Making Wise Decisions in the Midst of Endless Demands* (Nashville: Nelson, 2014).

6. David Crowder Band, "How He Loves," by John Mark McMillan, track 10 on *Church Music*, sixstepsrecords/Sparrow Records, 2009.

7. Brené Brown, *The Gifts of Imperfection: Let Go of Who You Think You're Supposed to Be and Embrace Who You Are* (Center City, MN: Hazelden, 2010), 56.

8. Malcolm Gladwell, *David and Goliath: Underdogs, Misfits, and the Art of Battling Giants* (New York: Little, Brown and Company, 2013).

9. Brown, *Gifts of Imperfection*, 73, 57.

10. C. S. Lewis, *The Lion, the Witch and the Wardrobe* (London: HarperCollins, 2015).

CHAPTER 10

1. Shauna Niequist, *Present Over Perfect: Leaving Behind Frantic for a Simpler, More Soulful Way of Living* (Grand Rapids, MI: Zondervan, 2016), 104, 130.

2. Horatio Spafford, "It Is Well with My Soul," 1873, public domain.

3. Daniel Siegel, "Flipping Your Lid," September 11, 2011, video, 7:27, www.heartmindonline.org/resources/daniel-siegel-flipping-your-lid.

4. See Kevin Leman, *It's Your Kid, Not a Gerbil: Creating a Happier & Less-Stressed Home* (Carol Stream, IL: Tyndale, 2011).

5. Richard A. Swenson, *Margin: Restoring Emotional, Physical, Financial, and Time Reserves to Overloaded Lives*, rev. ed. (Colorado Springs: NavPress, 2004).

6. Stuart Brown, quoted in Jennifer Wallace, "Why It's Good for Grown-Ups to Go Play," *Washington Post*, May 20, 2017, www.washingtonpost.com/national /health-science/why-its-good-for-grown-ups-to-go-play/2017/05/19/99810292 -fd1f-11e6-8ebe-6e0dbe4f2bca_story.

7. Brown, quoted in Wallace, "Why It's Good."

8. Sue C. Bratton et al., *Child Parent Relationship Therapy (CPRT) Treatment Manual: A 10-Session Filial Therapy Model for Training Parents* (New York: Routledge, 2006), 10.

9. Mother Teresa, quoted in Edward Le Joly and Jaya Chaliha, eds., *Reaching Out in Love: Stories Told by Mother Teresa* (New Delhi, India: Penguin, 1999), 142.

About the Author

Terra Mattson, MA, LMFT, LPC, is passionate about peeling away the layers that keep us from living loved and experiencing the fullness of grace. She's married to Jeff, who has been her best friend and business partner for the last two decades, and they are raising their two daughters on five acres of old-growth woods in the Oregon wine country.

Terra completed her master's in marriage and family therapy at George Fox University and is a licensed marriage and family therapist and licensed professional counselor. For the last fifteen years, she has run a thriving private practice, working with leaders, couples, individuals, youths, and families. Known for her trauma-informed expertise, she has provided counsel on everything from anxiety and abuse recovery to sex addiction and sexual betrayal recovery.

In 2011, Terra and her husband, Jeff, launched Living Wholehearted, a counseling and organizational-development firm that helps leaders live with integrity. As the clinical director, Terra oversees an amazing team of trauma-informed mental health professionals and leadership coaches. She has enjoyed speaking and writing, as well as leading retreats for women, couples, and leaders around the nation and at their Living Wholehearted Lodge & Retreat.

Inspired by their own daughters and sharpened by two decades in ministry, leadership, and mental health, Terra and her husband cofounded Courageous Girls, a global movement equipping moms to journey together at every stage of a daughters' growing years. She cohosts the *Living Wholehearted Podcast with Jeff and Terra Mattson*.

Terra loves camping, laughing, playing board games, and being with good friends. Between time with her girls, two golden retrievers, fifteen chickens, and a duck, Terra can be found sipping on a hemp caramel vanilla latte as she makes her way through the pile of books on her nightstand.

Follow Terra on Instagram (@terramattson) or visit her website, www.terramattson.com.

"Resilience and courage are not about being strong but about leaning into the One who is stronger than anything we could ever face."

—*Terra Mattson*

BE LOVED
LOVE WELL

What if you didn't have to raise your daughter alone? Courageous Girls is equipping moms with biblical and clinical wisdom for every stage of their daughters' growing years in order to raise up a generation of girls who are firmly rooted in grace, resiliency, and unwavering purpose.

The time is now.
Are you in?

Register for free today at www.mycourageousgirls.com